PUBERTY boy

Geoff Price

ALLEN&UNWIN

DEDICATION

**To my father Allan for his generosity in many things,
and my mother Marion for her care, with deep thanks.**

First published in 2005
Copyright © Geoff Price text 2005
Copyright © CKSD concept and design 2005

Allen & Unwin
83 Alexander Street
Crows Nest NSW 2065
Australia
Phone: (61 2) 8425 0100
Fax: (61 2) 9906 2218
Email: info@allenandunwin.com
Web: www.allenandunwin.com

National Library of Australia
Cataloguing-in-Publication entry is available.

ISBN 1 74114 563 5

PHOTOGRAPHY: Katrina Crook
ILLUSTRATIONS: **Jan Garben**
CARTOONS: **Sam Young**
THANKS TO SYDNEY INDOOR CLIMBING GYM
extra photographs by Giacomo Bianchina: pages 5, 51, 64, 78
and Luke Todaro: page 111
Some of the graffiti that appears in the photography is the work of K-Agent and Gonzo

Set in 10/15 pt TheMix by Seymour Designs
Printed by Everbest Printing Co. Ltd., China

10 9 8 7 6 5 4 3 2

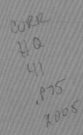

ACKNOWLEDGMENTS

Writing this book has been a satisfying adventure back into my own puberty, into the present puberty world of many boys, and memories of hundreds of men, colleagues, friends and clients. It has been a privilege and loads of laughs and fun. I just wish someone had written *Puberty Boy* for me when I was a young teen!

This book would not have been possible without my colleagues at Pathways to Manhood, Don Bowak, Paul Henley, Ranald Allan, Allan Rudner, Bere, Joseph Raya, Garry Thompson and especially Arne Rubinstein. Thank you for your friendship, stories, your passion over the years to help boys become young men, and for your eldership, wisdom downloads, feedback and inspiration in so many ways. You all deserve a huge honouring for the difference  you have made, and continue to make, to thousands of boys' and families' lives. I am grateful to each of you, the book owes much to you all.

Rex Finch, John Taylor, Rob Goodridge and George Burkitt have told their stories in our men's group for over ten years—you have all enriched the book.

Puberty Boys Giacomo Bianchino, Harrison Brown, Harrison Checkley, Will Marshall, Trystan Richards, Luke Todaro, Julian Chai, Chadd Knights, Glynn-Jakeb Emery, Alex Latham, Varvn Fernando and Jack Kelly all played a vital part saying what they wanted in the book and reading the drafts! Thanks also to Carla Todaro and Sara Marshall for their contribution.

Special thanks to Chris Price who gave insightful counsel, support and encouragement. Wendy Pettit, Tony Carlon, Jonathan Dallwitz, Roger Nelson, Marybeth Zang, Shushann Movsessian, Maree Lipschitz, Annelies Kaufman all helped in valuable ways, many very personal! Dr Michael Lowy and Dr George Burkitt reviewed the drafts using their vast medical expertise to improve the book. David Mowaljarli and Timmy Burrarwanga both helped me to understand more deeply about the principles of indigenous rites of passage and initiation and their importance for all young men.

Thanks also to Di Todaro and Liz Seymour of CKSD; illustrator Jan Garben, cartoonist Sam Young and photographer Katrina Crook; editor Alex Nahlous, publisher Annette Barlow and the team at Allen & Unwin, who brought their creativity, support and belief in the book.

In the end the book has come together with direct and not-so-direct contributions from many people, men and women with lots of different talents, who, like me, care about boys becoming healthy young men. Puberty and teen years are like the table legs that hold up healthy adulthood. May your table legs be strong. I hope *Puberty Boy* has the same kind of value for you as it has for me.

Lastly, if you enjoyed *Puberty Boy*, if it made sense to you, I'd like to hear from you. Please let me know by writing to me care of Allen & Unwin Publishers, 83 Alexander St Crows Nest, NSW 2065 or by email to geoff@talkitover.info.

CONTENTS

Chapter 1

Welcome to
PUBERTY BOY!

I can still remember when I was 10, walking home from school one day with two friends from class. They were talking about sex, where babies came from, erections and stuff. I was so surprised! I didn't know about any of that stuff and I remember thinking: 'Tell me more, tell me more!'. I didn't say too much so they wouldn't notice, but I was burning with curiosity.

A while later my mum announced that there was a 'father and son night' on at the town hall and I would be going with Dad. I thought, 'As if!'. But there was no way out of it and I found myself sitting there embarrassed next to my dad, listening to an old lady with blue hair rave on and put up slides of hens, roosters, eggs and chickens. We had to pretty much put two and two together and imagine what people do. There was no talking about erections, penises, zits, pubic hair, masturbation, semen, testicles and all the juicy stuff that I was bursting to know about. We boys were still pretty much in the dark.

Even today, parents and teachers are sometimes uncomfortable talking about puberty issues or have their own no-go areas or blind spots. And if you're relying on the guys at school to explain it all, they can give you the wrong information and confuse you.

So let me say straight up: I won't be talking in riddles about chickens and eggs at any time in this book. I'm going to give you accurate info about your body, and this puberty thing, that you need for your journey from boy to young man … and believe me there's a lot more to it than just body changes!

Why should I read about puberty you ask? Because it's one of the most important and interesting things you could ever do. And you won't have to plough through trillions of pages of boring stuff either. Throughout *Puberty Boy*, I've included boys' 🙂 and men's 🙂 real stories about puberty that will make reading so much better, and there's a glossary at the back with the meaning of all the new words I've used in the book in **bold**, so you can easily flip over to check out a new word.

Boys' and men's real stories about puberty

I've taken hundreds of Puberty Boys and their dads on wilderness camps. What boys say they want is to hear men's puberty stories, of happy, funny and tough times, just the way it really happened. So I've asked many Puberty Boys, older teens, young men and older men to tell their honest puberty stories to welcome you into the community of men. Puberty Boys' stories will have this symbol and Men's stories will have the symbol like this one below.

I wish my father had talked to me about some of the things that would happen to me physically and emotionally during puberty. I can't remember him talking to me at all, it just happened and if I learnt anything it was from the other kids. When I was 12, we had a sex lecture at school. It was a woman who came in and I remember her talking about French letters, which is now condoms, and she took one out and I remember the whole class giggling, giggling, giggling …

These stories will help you to find new ways of looking at things, to think and act in new, grown-up man kind of ways. They will help you to become more aware of, and develop, new potentials in you, and help you to make better choices, increase your personal power and meet your challenges. The idea is that you'll know yourself inside and out by the time you put *Puberty Boy* down.

Boys are born, men are made!

The good news is that you are not the first to face the challenges of puberty. For thousands of years in all cultures, Puberty Boys have been guided by the elders in their communities who taught them knowledge of puberty and being a man. This is what boys' initiations are really about. They pass on the knowledge that boys need at that stage, and that's what this book is all about, knowledge to help you understand and make the most of this growing time in your life. **Boys are born, men are made**. Healthy manhood doesn't happen by accident. *Puberty Boy*'s message is that you can choose what kind of man you want to be.

Adults, believe it or not, have been through puberty before you. You heard right! Every adult walking the earth has been through puberty. They've been there with the pimples and the aches and pains of growing. Talking to them is one of the best ways to get more information, troubleshoot problems you might come across and decide about the kind of Puberty Boy, and later man, that you want to be. If you can talk to your mother and father, that's great. Sometimes they're not around or are difficult to talk to. Then it's best to find older brothers, uncles, people you trust, grandfathers, other relatives, teachers, school counsellors or mentors to speak to. **It takes more courage to ask questions and talk about our problems than to say nothing or shut them away.**

Puberty Boy is for you to read before, during and after puberty. Some things may be hard to understand today but in a little while, it might be just what you need to know ... it's your body, your life, so let's discover ...

Chapter 2

PUBERTY
what is it and when?

You've already achieved amazing things growing from a baby (congratulations!). All that growing and learning in childhood ... and then comes puberty! It's pronounced PYU–BER–TEE, and it is a word from old English and Latin meaning the time when boys and girls become sexually mature and physically able to reproduce. For us males that's being able to father a baby.

Puberty is the time when you grow and change more and faster than at any time of your life except when you were a baby. But not only is it a time of major bodily changes, it's the time you begin to make the **thinking shift** from boy to young man, make the break from childhood that leads to **adolescence** ... it's a time when you're not a child any more, but you're not yet a grown-up. It's a time of challenges!

And guess what, the two big challenges of puberty are ones you've already been working on successfully since you were little: becoming even more **independent** and being more **self-responsible**. So you've already proved you can do it! Only now, at puberty, it's time to step these up to another level, those of a young man, not a boy.

Independence means doing and thinking more for yourself, depending more on yourself and less on your parents and other people. Like washing your own clothes.

Responsibility (we can think of this as response-ability) is your ability to think, manage, be more in charge of yourself, act and respond on your own, and more like a man. Like making your own decisions by thinking it through yourself, then doing what you decide.

 Puberty is all about changes to your body and changes to friends. I reckon life's about enjoying yourself and doing something good. I went through lots of stages like fashion and hobbies, some have come back, some haven't. I went through a really crazy stage of wanting to kill ants ... and just mad about keeping fish in tanks.

Brrrrrring ... your inner alarm clock goes off

So, when does it all start? Do you like sit around waiting for the hair on your chest to start growing? Well, not exactly, but sort of!

At around age 11 to 12, you'll start to see changes in your body. This happens a little later in boys than in girls, and boys mature more slowly and unevenly! Some boys start earlier than 11, some later than 12. Everyone's different, so you'll have your own starting time. Remember, you're unique, so there's no one right timetable. For some it takes a year for body changes to happen, others six years, so you'll notice some friends stay short and some suddenly become tall. At puberty, your body starts to grow faster than at any other time in your life, except your very first year—this time though, you'll have to feed and dress yourself. Your body will change shape and grow in special ways as it takes on sexual characteristics. You will see, feel and experience changes that can be exciting, terrific, welcome, embarrassing, confusing, wonderful, frightening and much more.

Your body is amazing and wonderful. It knows the right time and pace to start changing for you.

Testosterone kicks off your changes

When the time is right for you, your brain kicks off the changes by sending signals to your testicles, the factories in your scrotum (we'll say more on this one a little later) that make chemicals called hormones (pronounced HOR-MOANS). Hormones are the things that create changes in you.

Testosterone (it's fantastic stuff!), pronounced TES-TOS-TER-OWN, is the main rocket-fuel hormone in us fellas that can take you on a roller coaster ride and change everything—your body, hair, voice, even your penis. Remember, it happens to everyone in the whole world. Every guy you know—whether he's an old dude or a teenager, has been through puberty. There's no way you can grow up without it.

Your puberty timetable

Puberty starts and continues with your hormones controlling the show. But, how well you eat, as in, what you put inside your body, and what is happening with your emotions, friends and family life also affect when puberty starts and how long it lasts. Changes in your body can happen very slowly or very quickly. Sometimes everything slows down (like when you feel like you've had the same zit in the exact same spot for a month!), sometimes there are growth spurts (like when you come to school one day and realise your best friend is suddenly taller than you!).

A guide to when Puberty Boys' growth spurts start and finish:									
Growth spurts	10	11	12	13	14	15	16	17	18
Testicles & scrotum		x	x	x	x	x			
Pubic hair		x	x	x	x				
Penis			x	x	x	x			
Hands, feet, ears		x	x	x	x	x	x		
Height, upper body			x	x	x	x	x	x	
Voice			x	x	x	x	x	x	x
Armpit & facial hair					x	x	x	x	x

(The development stages in the table and information in this book are intended as guidelines only. Each person is unique and will develop at their own pace and at their own time.)

Puberty is about body changes, physical appearance, getting pimples and stuff. I'm wanting to look after how I look more and I am starting to care more about which clothes I wear. I want to look good to impress girls …

Everyone's different and unique and that's OK!

Some Puberty Boys may start to compare their bodies with their friends' or people at school, and they might start to become worried about the differences they see.

The three most common things that worry boys at puberty are:
◎ height;
◎ their lack of pubic hair when the early developing boys have pubes;
◎ and that their penis is smaller than other boys'.

The last one is a biggie. Even young men whose penis was, and is, above average size also worry about this! Is my penis size normal, is it big enough? That's the 6-million-dollar question most boys (and some men) wonder and worry about! We'll put pubes and penis questions on the noticeboard for later in the book, chapter 4, page 26.

If your body is going slow, or fast, with the whole development business, it helps to remember that your development timetable is something you inherit, like the colour of your hair and eyes. This means that your father and grandfather were probably the same way, and that there's nothing you can do to speed it up when your voice breaks or slow it down when you grow taller. If it worries you, talking to your father or grandfather about it might help. You might be surprised by how much they have to tell you.

If you've noticed that you are developing a bit later than others, what do you think Puberty Boys who develop early worry about? Yep, you got it, they have the opposite problem. They're worried they are too tall or have hairs when no-one else does, or could be wishing that their hairs would stop growing so quickly!

Difference between us is sooo necessary! If everyone was the same, we'd look like really freaky robots! This guy I know, he was smaller than everyone else. He seemed to be one of the last boys to go through puberty. He felt so different from all the others, and he was just terrified

I was so different, the skinniest boy in my class. I just trusted that I must be skinny for a good reason. I felt better when I made lists of all the parts of my body that I really liked and stuck it on the wall. I would sometimes ask my parents what they loved about my body, turns out they loved my long hands the best!

Did you know ...
Testis is the proper medical name for one of your balls. Testes is the plural— that's two balls! In this book I'll use the common word testicle, or testicles, 'cause that's the word most people know and use.

I think puberty is lots of things, chemical changes causing physical and mental changes, all sorts of things. Hair grows in different regions besides your head, your voice breaks, there's testosterone ... a bit more aggression ... bring back the biff kind of stuff.

When people say things about my body I can feel hurt or embarrassed ... I've learnt that I may have got the meaning wrong! So I need to check out what they meant. Anyway a healthy man is proud of himself and his body just as it is. He never feels ashamed of his own body.

that he was really small. It wasn't so bad when he was 12, but it got really bad at 13 and 14. Even in footy, it got to the stage where he had to play to his weight which was a team way below the other boys his age. But then he realised that in cricket, it wasn't done on weight so his height and size didn't matter. He became the captain of the cricket team! That helped.

This guy told me recently that if only he'd been able to realise, at the time, that being so small was actually a gift, that later in life it would enable him to understand the feelings of people who didn't fit in and be kinder to them, that would have helped him hugely! So maybe his experience can help you to find the positive sides of any difficulty you may have.

So if you're worried about being different to other boys think about this stuff for a while:

1. Differences usually even out by the end of puberty, till then ...
2. Remember that what others think of you is their stuff, not your business.
3. You have a choice about seeing yourself positively or negatively.
4. Make a list of your positive features. Stick it up on your wall and read it daily.
5. Stop comparing yourself to, and competing with, others. Accept yourself for the wonderful person that you are.
6. Your qualities and personality are more important to others than your appearance.

Differences do even out

It doesn't matter if you start first or finish last—eventually everyone catches up, and by the time we're 16 or 17 we've done most of our physical growing and developing. I know it sounds impossible to believe now, when what you want most in the world is to fit in with your peers (that's boys your own age), and not be **different**, but remember this

One year there was only one guy with pubic hair, it was all over him, armpits, legs, everywhere. The next year everything changed. There were acres of pubic hair and a few guys with dicks that made most of the skinny guys like me feel awkward. And guys got teased basically. I remember one guy who wouldn't take off his underwear, no matter what, he wore it in the shower he was so embarrassed.

I got pubic hair well before anyone else in my class. I didn't know why and I became very self-conscious and tried to hide it from the others. I look back now and I can understand that I was just an early developer, but at the time I just wanted to be like the others, it didn't seem like anything to be proud of. It's quite funny really because I was bald on my head by the time I was 23. I had it first down there, and lost it first up here!

when you are feeling too short or too tall, or your voice is too high or too low: **that's the way it is with our bodies and there's no right way or wrong way to look at it.**

Puberty is a time when we can become super aware of our bodies—we can wish we were different or more like someone else. Every boy wishes to be on the half-way line, tall boys wish they were shorter, short boys wish they were taller, everyone wants to be in the middle of everyone else.

What're you laughing at?

I was 12, riding my skateboard down the hill and going so fast that I got the deathwobbles. I knew I was going to stack it, and I did, I scraped down the road on my bum, and got the biggest gravel rash you've ever seen. It was from my bum, half way down my thigh, so deep there were actual bits of gravel stuck in it. It was so painful I ran home crying, just howling like a dog, and my mum took me into the bathroom and took my pants off and she's looking at my gravel rash, picking bits of rock out of it, then all of sudden she starts laughing and I said, 'What are you laughing at Mum?' and she goes, 'Oh, it's so cute, you've got a little pubic hair'. I didn't even know that I had it, so my mum found my first pubic hair and she laughed. I was so embarrassed, and that was the last time she'd see me without my underwear. I would never let her come into the bathroom after that.

Have you had something similar happen with your mum or older brother or sister? Did they see some of your pubic hair and do something like laugh or giggle? We can be so sensitive at puberty, and we can get embarrassed so easily. And it's sooo easy to take things personally, and make the mistake of thinking that others are laughing **AT US**, rather than laughing **WITH US**. Maybe this mum could have been a bit more sensitive. What she was probably feeling was happiness at the sight of her son's first pubic hair, the first external sign of her son becoming a man. His mum called it cute, but he freaked out. His mum felt close to him, but he misunderstood her meaning. Because he was so sensitive, he then hid himself from her forever. This is a trap that we can avoid if we are aware of it.

For me puberty is all about changing into an adult, but to do that I have to make many changes in different ways, like maturing more.

Chapter 3

CHANGES
on every front

What is happening to my body?

So what will actually happen to you during puberty? There'll be changes on every front, and back, and top and bottom—so don't freak out. If you've started noticing that things are changing, this is a great sign that puberty is happening just as it should, that you are on track.

But just hang on for a minute—let's take a little detour to see the big picture of body changes.

First signs to look out for

The only body system that doesn't start functioning until you hit puberty is your reproductive (or sexual) system. So if you thought that the body changes of puberty are mostly about getting your body ready for its future sexual function, you're spot on.

Your gonads (no, not goannas) wake up

At about age 8 or 9 special hormones silently go between your brain and your gonads. The **gonads** (GO–NADS) are the male and female primary sex organs. In females it's the **ovaries** and in males the **testicles** or balls. Before these hormones wake up your testicles, they are basically in one big snooze. But as soon as they're awake, they start to enlarge and get busy developing special cells to make hormones.

About two years later, your testicles begin to produce and release sex hormones, mainly testosterone, and this brings on the puberty changes to the max.

While this stuff is being silently produced (don't expect to hear any banging going on), you'll notice that your testicles and scrotum will start to grow bigger, and some pubic hair will start to grow. About a year later your penis starts to grow longer and thicker for about two years.

Head, hands and feet grow up first

There are also other visible changes that are not essential for sex or reproduction but that make you different from, and attractive to, the other sex (hooray!): the shape and size of your body, body hair and voice pitch. Your head, hands and feet reach adult proportion first, so they might look oversize for a while. Arms, legs, hands, feet and ears may grow faster than the rest of your body. You may feel gawky, clumsy and trip over things as your body adjusts to its new dimensions!

Growth and other spurts

There will be all kinds of spurts during puberty! Your legs and arms will get longer and suddenly there may be a gap between your socks and your long pants, or your sleeves don't come to your wrists. Your legs will stop growing out of your trousers about a year before you will grow out of your shirt sleeves.

Then you start to take on a new more angular shape—you'll start to look like the men around you—your upper chest starts to get bigger and your shoulders broader. You'll also start to gain a lot of weight, because your bones become heavier and you'll get a lot more muscle bulk. During the peak year of your growth spurt, usually around 14, you may shoot up between 6–12 centimetres. That's huge!

Man-boobs?

You might even notice swelling under your nipples that looks like you're growing breasts. Before you start freaking out, let me assure you, you won't turn into a woman! It's quite common, normal and usually short-lived. This happens because fat gets laid down in the breast ... that's just the way it is for some boys, it's a genetic thing. Boys who don't like their chest this way may be embarrassed and they might not like to take their shirts off, or avoid swimming. If this happens to you and it worries you, it can be treated. Talk to your parents and doctor about it.

Pubes ... nature's advertisement!

Before puberty you will have fine, light-coloured hair growing on your body called vellus. At puberty your vellus hair starts to get thicker and pubic hair starts to grow around your penis and scrotum. (A couple of years later you'll start getting facial and armpit hair too.) Pubes are really important—it's true! They exist to protect your soft sensitive bits from water, dust, dirt, insect bites, cold breezes and other things, and help keep them nice and warm.

Pubes are nature's advertisement, like a huge neon sign, saying to others, 'Hey you, look at me, I'm physically ready to make babies, pay attention!' Now having pubes doesn't mean that we are really ready to be a father, but it sends the first visual signals to others.

There's more! Pubes, armpit and body hair do something else that's really important. Your sweat glands develop during puberty, and when you sweat you produce your natural personal scent (called pheromones) to attract others by smell. Your body hair catches this scent and helps others notice your smell. Human's sense of smell connects big time to our sexual instincts and responses, that's why some women wear perfume and some men aftershave: On the other hand, if you don't shower enough and change your dirty undies and socks daily, bacteria grow in the sweat and produce body odour (BO), and this my friends is not particularly pleasant, and there's not likely to be much attraction. It might be that people run a mile when they smell you coming!

Pubes usually start putting in an appearance at around 11–12 years, for some it may start at 14 or a little older. You may start with just one solitary hair, usually in the pubic area, on the skin above and close to the base of your penis, then more hair will start spreading slowly. Hair may grow later on the base of the shaft of your penis, but otherwise it won't grow on the penis itself. Some hairs do grow on the scrotum and around behind the scrotum on the **perineum** (the skin area between your scrotum and your anus) and around to the anus which will usually have some hair around it later. First hairs may be straightish, but later on your pubes will get kinks and lots of curls.

Body hair will grow too and may extend up from the pubic area and down the inside of your legs. In some guys a line of pubic hair can come right up the belly to the belly button, and it can extend to join up with chest hair. Some guys have almost no chest hair, some have a jungle.

Pubic hair can be various colours, but you'll know what to expect by the colour of hair on your head. If you have ginger hair, you'll probably have pubic hair to match. If yours is snowy you'll most likely have light-coloured pubes to match. Mostly though, pubic hair is black or dark brown.

Body hair doesn't grow in one hit. It may keep growing on your arms, legs, back of hands, armpits, shoulders, bottom, chest and back, up till you are around 20. The amount, thickness, colour and where this hair grows differs from one man to the next because guess what? We're all different. We will likely (but not always) have similar body and beard hair to our dad, but even brothers can be different.

I've just started high school ... some boys mature early, some really beef it up and nearly play in the first fifteen. Then there are people like me who are just starting puberty. I get called baldy and things like that because I haven't got any pubes ... I don't know how they'd know, but they get it into their head that if you're smaller than them that you're a baldy.

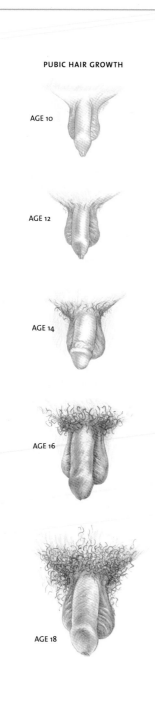

PUBIC HAIR GROWTH

AGE 10

AGE 12

AGE 14

AGE 16

AGE 18

From bum fluff to beard

You won't have a beard until you're close to the end of puberty. At first, it'll be soft and very sparse, but it gets more and more dense as the hairs multiply and each one gets thicker. Some people have heavy beards, some light beards. Shaving can start any time you feel like it, or you can just let it grow. If you don't like the soft bum fluff that grows at first you can shave it off. Sometimes chin or upper lip hair can be thicker than on the cheeks and there may be light or bald patches! It's nice to make a big celebration and have a bit of fun with your family standing around when you have your first shave milestone. Talk to your dad or older brother or cousin about when they decided to start shaving. See if you're really ready for it.

Shaving your beard

Most people use razors with blades. These razors have blade heads that you throw away when they get too blunt. While you're shaving, rinse out the hairs caught in the blades a few times. This helps keep the blade clean and do the job properly. The older the blade you use, the more little nicks in your skin! The heavier the beard, the shorter the blade life.

Blades need a lubricant to run smoothly over the skin. You can buy shaving lather cream, use soap, or experiment with skin moisturisers, like sorbolene. Soap does dry out skin so you should see what suits your skin type.

Some people use electric razors. You don't wet your face or use lubricants with an electric razor. It's best to read the instructions of any electrical equipment so that you know you're using it properly.

We each have to experiment to find what suits us best. Maybe you will choose a mo or beard. What do the men around you have? Do you think you'd like to look more like them or find something that suits your personality? Talk to your dad or brother about what sort of shaver they use and hey, why not get them to show you how to do it?

Testie-pops ... Voiiiccce Breaaaaaakkkkks

There's another change that will take place too: testosterone makes your vocal chords become longer and thicker and as this happens your voice starts to sound deeper and lower. Voice changes can start during early puberty and should be completed by mid- to late puberty. In the meantime, your voice may sometimes 'crack' (that's a testie-pop), that is, jump up and down in pitch. You might be saying something, and suddenly your voice starts becoming really high or low! This is why it's called your voice 'breaking'.

When the vocal chords reach their adult length (about age 15–18), the cracking will stop and your voice will be permanently lower.

I was a late developer. I can remember going to university at 18, someone remarked that the hair on my chin was slower growing than my moustache. That was the first time I thought about it. I'm pretty hairy now.

21

Stretch marks, pimples ... what more can I deal with?

With all this rapid body and muscle growth your skin may struggle in places to grow fast enough to keep up, so it might stretch and leave 'stretch marks' visible on your skin.

Your mother, or other adult women in your life, may know about stretch marks as it often happens to women during puberty around the breast area and when their baby is growing fast inside them and the skin over the tummy has to stretch. If the skin isn't elastic enough, and it can't stretch fast enough, then stretch marks will appear. If this happens the marks might fade later so you'll hardly notice them, but they might always be there.

For us boys, the thigh, upper leg and buttock muscles are the most likely places where muscles may grow so fast that the skin can't keep up. We can help our skin a little by keeping it supple (to keep its elasticity) and moist with moisturiser.

Another common thing that happens to your skin, usually around age 13 or 14, is that the oil glands in the skin grow and may become overactive and clogged. The result can be pimples and even acne. Pimples and acne can happen on your body but the face is where it happens most, shows the most, and where we can be most sensitive to it because it affects our looks. I've got a lot more info on pimples for you on pages 64–6.

Inside developments too!

OK so we've checked out what you can see on the outside, but there are developments inside your reproductive system and head too.

Once in puberty mode, your testicles (or balls), not only make testosterone, but also **spermatozoa** (pronounced SPERM-AT-O-ZOA, but we'll call them **sperm** for short). Sperm can create a baby if they fertilise an egg waiting inside a woman's body, then the baby starts to grow in the **uterus** of the woman.

These new hormones in your blood also start the maturation of the structures and tubes that will care for and carry the sperm, and these produce the fluid that sperm swim in, that's **semen** (I'll tell you more about semen later). These tubes and structures, called the **epididymis** (EPI-DID-EE-MISS), **ejaculatory ducts** (EE-JAK-ULAY-TORY) and the **urethra** (YOU-REETH-RAR) start to grow too. Reproductive glands, like the seminal vesicles, prostate and the **bulbourethral glands**, mature too. I'll tell you more about all these on page 37.

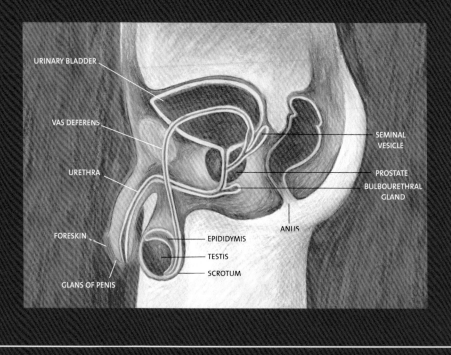

URINARY BLADDER

VAS DEFERENS

URETHRA

SEMINAL VESICLE

PROSTATE

BULBOURETHRAL GLAND

ANUS

FORESKIN

EPIDIDYMIS

TESTIS

SCROTUM

GLANS OF PENIS

The sperm and semen are produced so that the erect **penis** can deliver semen, containing millions of sperm into a woman's vagina, from where they swim like mad, some stronger than others, up into the woman's uterus and fallopian tubes, hunting for an egg. One successful sperm meets an egg, and this is called **fertilisation**, and it is the creation of a baby.

Our thinking changes as well

So much is going on with your body that is visible on the outside that we may not notice that there are many things changing inside our heads and hearts too. Changes to how we think and feel about things and people are really important during puberty, and for some people, it can take over everything else going on in life!

You might start to feel different about your family, friends and classmates. You might start to see what they do in a new light or have new ideas. The girl who was getting on your nerves yesterday might suddenly look cute enough to make you think, 'hmm, I want to be her friend'! You may start to look and think about yourself a lot more and wonder where you fit in the world—yeah, I know, that's a biggie, but it happens! You may care more about what people think of you and have a growing need to want to belong with your friends and be accepted and liked. You'll naturally start to want to spend less time with your parents and more with people your own age. You may want to change your clothes and the way you dress and the things you'll be interested in talking about will change.

All this is part of becoming yourself, and an adult. As we grow, we start to become more aware of what is going on around us and we change as we respond to our friends becoming more adult too. **That's response-ability!**

Chapter 4

EXPLORING
your body

Close-up tour of your genitals

Genitals (pronounced JEN-IT-ALS) is the word for your reproductive organs and it comes from the same word origin as genius, generate and genesis, all words about creation, which seems right because that's what our genitals can do, **create new life**.

I've included an illustration of the genital area because it's good to get to know your own body. You can do this by taking a close look at your own genital area, that's the whole pubic area where your penis and balls are between your legs. But please, don't confuse pubic area with public area! You definitely need privacy for this.

Start by finding a hand mirror and choosing a quiet time, in a private place like the bathroom or your bedroom where you can close the door, relax and make sure you won't be interrupted. A hand mirror is great because it allows you to have a close look at the whole area. You can even use your fingers to move things around so you can look under things and from different angles. Be gentle, and don't do anything that hurts. You can also use your fingers just to check out the different textures. Take a close look at everything interesting to you.

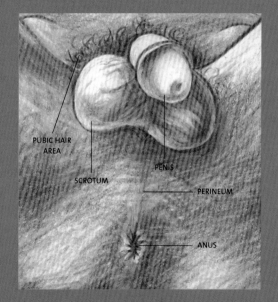

PUBIC HAIR
AREA

PENIS

SCROTUM

PERINEUM

ANUS

Perineum: Pubic bone to tail bone

Above your penis is the pubic bone. The perineum is the whole area between the pubic bone and your coccyx or tail bone behind your anus. If you press your fingers into the perineum skin just behind your balls, towards your anus, you will be able to feel the base of your penis, its root, where it extends into your pelvis.

In the freezing showers on camp, I'd look at my groin, as you do, and it's all disappeared! Just a mass of hair and there's nothing there! It's because they come straight up into the stomach it's so cold.

If it's cold, that's spanner weather because your nuts tighten up so much you need a spanner to undo them.

Did you know ...

Watch your scrotum closely ... it looks like a bag of worms! You'll notice that it's always moving and changing shape a little. This helps with air circulation.

Scrotum ... like a bag of worms!

Your scrotum holds your testicles. The skin texture of your scrotum may be different in places. At puberty the scrotum skin becomes thicker and darkens to be a more red-brown colour, and becomes more sensitive to touch. Scrotum skin can be more dark for people of certain races. At different times, the scrotum can be loose or tight.

The scrotum's job is to enclose, protect, support and hold the testicles in the right place relative to your body. This is mainly to keep them at the right temperature for them to produce sperm. Sperm need just the right temperature, which is about 35°C (95°F). The scrotum and the muscles around it manage the temperature of the testicles by themselves, without you having to do anything. If it's warm, the skin will be loose and hanging down, and if it's cold, the scrotum will tighten up and move the testicles closer to the body.

The scrotum also tightens up and holds the balls close to the body when we have an erection and are getting ready to ejaculate. This is part of the process of allowing the semen to move through the tubes at the right time. So the scrotum is pretty amazing, always changing, automatically doing its job without us being aware of it.

Along the midline of the scrotum, there's a ridge in the skin that goes all the way from your anus to the underside of your penis. This is called the **raphe** (pronounced RAFE). This is where the skin closed up as you were developing in the womb. The scrotum sac is divided vertically into two compartments, one for each testicle, so that infection in one will not generally affect the other.

Mention scrotums and boys usually groan, say yuk and stuff. But they can be quite useful for male-only party tricks like the 'bee sting' ... this is when you stretch your scrotum and one testicle beyond the lower regions of your underdaks, squeezing the skin tight around the testicle and pressing the tackle against your leg, and say to your friends ... 'hey have you seen my bee sting?'. When they realise what it is they are staring at they burst out laughing.

Testicles (inside the bag)

You've normally got two testicles inside your scrotum. Usually the left testicle hangs just a little lower in the scrotum than the other so that the two are not as likely to be bashed together, like when a cricket ball comes flying at you. Anyone who has ever received a cricket ball or even a bump in the nuts will tell you, testicles are very, **very sensitive**. They can take punishment, but they are delicate things, so it pays to wear a box or jock strap if they are likely to get pounded.

Testicles have two main jobs in life: to produce sperm, and produce androgens, male sex hormones, the main one being testosterone. There are special different cells in the testicles to do these jobs.

Testicles start to grow to their full size at the start of puberty. Because everyone is different, there is a wide range of adult testicle size that is considered normal.

Testes are ovals, adult size is about 4 cm (1½ inches) long by 2.5 cm (1 inch) wide, each weighs about 10–14 gram (¼-½ oz). The average volume of a testicle of an adult Western male is between 15 and 25 millilitres (½–1 fl oz), you can see from the drawings roughly how big testicles are at various stages of growth.

Doctors generally agree that the bigger the balls the more sperm you will produce. But like everything about us, there are no strict rules. Some infertile men have large testicles and some men with many children have smallish ones, so fertility is not all about the size of the testicles. If a testicle is lost, say by accident, men can still father a baby with one testicle.

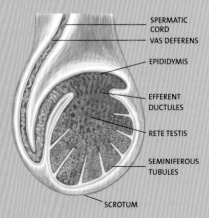

TESTIS, CROSS SECTION

SPERMATIC CORD
VAS DEFERENS
EPIDIDYMIS
EFFERENT DUCTULES
RETE TESTIS
SEMINIFEROUS TUBULES
SCROTUM

ACTUAL TESTICULAR SIZE

YOUNG BOY   PRE-PUBERTY   ADULT

Did you know ...
Some body builders and athletes take anabolic steroids—this is like overdosing on testosterone, and it has a special danger. If we take in too much testosterone the feedback loop from the brain kicks in, resulting in less production of other hormones, and without these your testicles shrink!

Testosterone ... a boy's own hormone

Testosterone, is made by special cells in the testicles, and is the main male sex hormone that is crucial for you to grow as a man.

Sperm—those tadpole thingies!

A sperm is a super sophisticated structure that contains thousands of **genes** (JEENS). Inside each mature testicle is about 100–150 metres of tiny tubes (called **seminiferous tubules**) that carry semen. These tubes are lined with cells that produce the sperm. As you mature they make more, so that by the time you're through puberty, your testicles churn out 50–100 million little tadpole warriors every day. You'll produce sperm for the rest of your life, but it will get slower when you get old.

It takes 70 days for sperm to look like tadpoles! They start out as small round cells, but they turn into the tadpole shape because they need to swim. It's all in the tail! It wags and lashes to help the sperm make its way up to an egg that's waiting in a woman's fallopian tube. If they can't swim, they can't get to the egg to fertilise it.

Sperm have a head and neck as well as a tail. Each little sperm has an 'engine' or energy store behind its neck, and this gives it the energy to swim. The head of the sperm contains all of a man's genetic material.

When sperm leave the tubules, they can't move or swim and wouldn't know an egg if they tripped over one! They move along into the epididymis which lies against the back of the testicle inside the scrotum, and it's here that each sperm undergoes about a week of final mission training in swimming, egg-seeking and penetrating skills. When it's finished training, it's declared fully qualified to fertilise an egg.

The epididymis runs down the back of the testicle from top to bottom. When they're ready to go, the sperm are all kept in the tail of the epididymis ready to be pushed along and eventually out—this is called an **ejaculation**. I'll explain more about ejaculation on page 40.

As the sperm leave the epididymis and are pushed through the

WORDS FOR TESTICLES
BALLS, NUTS, KNACKERS, EGGS, BOULDERS, NADS, ROCKS, STONES, FAMILY JEWELS, GONGS, GOOLIES, OYSTERS

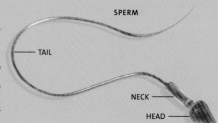

SPERM

TAIL

NECK

HEAD

different tubes and glands, these tubes and glands add fluids to the sperm. This fluid mixture is called **semen**. During ejaculation, the muscle waves push the semen into the **urethra** (where urine comes out) and they finally spurt out of the penis.

Not all sperm are perfect. If you look at them through a microscope about 20 per cent have abnormal form. They can have really big heads, or really small heads, or heads that don't look like heads at all! They can also have two tails, so they can't swim normally. The ones with two tails have no reproductive value.

Did you know ... The sperm's ability to fertilise an egg depends not just on how many sperm are produced, but also on whether it's able to swim, how strong it is and if it can squirm its way into the female's egg if it gets there first. It's first in wins! Only one sperm can penetrate and fertilise a woman's egg. Once that first one enters, the egg locks all the other sperm out.

SO WHAT HAPPENS TO ALL THE SPERM THAT DOESN'T GET PUSHED OUT OF THE BODY? In the sperm ducts, sperm can stay fertile for a few months just waiting for action. If they are not ejaculated, or pushed out of the body, they don't just build up until you burst, they eventually degenerate and are absorbed into the blood.

SPERM FERTILISING AN EGG

SPERM BREAKING THROUGH TO OVUM WHEN ONE SPERM HAS PENETRATED THE OVUM, NO OTHER SPERM CAN

Semen—it's not a sailing crew!

Semen is the fluid that comes out of the hole in the end of the erect penis when we ejaculate. It holds millions of invisible sperm in every drop.

Semen is a whitish, milky, pearly colour. It's very slippery and has a consistency like some shampoo, but it's not as thick. When it lands on skin after being pushed out, it'll sit there in dollops, so it's not as thin as water, but it will run downhill on sloping skin.

WHY IS SEMEN SUCH A BLOB?

Semen includes fibrin, the same stuff that helps make your blood clot. Fibrin helps semen stay in a blob, and stay at the top of the vagina initially after ejaculation, where sperm are in the best position to swim up to the egg. After a little while outside the male reproductive tract semen de-clots and goes runny.

It's all sticky and smelly?

Semen can be sticky stuff, not like glue but somehow little bits seem to manage to get everywhere. If some gets in your hair (it happens!) and dries out, your hair sets like it has gel in it. It dries up quite quickly and disappears; it doesn't stain, but will form a crusty powder. It can leave a kind of spot on sheets or other materials. It washes out easily in water.

Semen has a smell too, but it's harder to describe. Some people have said it smells a bit like alfalfa sprouts!

When we ejaculate there is usually about a teaspoon to a tablespoon full of semen each time. If we have ejaculated recently, there will be less semen the next time.

Did you know ...

When mature, your body makes about 1000 sperm in the time it takes for a heartbeat! 200 of the little fellas laid end to end are a centimetre long; 20 000 laid head to tail would make a metre.

YOU MIGHT HAVE HEARD OTHER NAMES FOR SEMEN LIKE
SEMINAL FLUID, CUM, BABY BATTER, JISM, JIS OR SPOOF!

Penis ... everything you ever wanted to know!

Now that we've talked about the things around, inside and that come out of the penis, it's time to take a look at the penis itself. By the way, that's the thing dangling with your balls!

Your penis is made for two main things: to urinate (pee) and to become erect when you are sexually aroused. A penis in its usual state is called **flaccid**, (pronounced FLASS-ID) meaning soft and droopy, or limp. Your penis will go hard and stiff and stand up. This is called an **erection**. Your penis will become erect when it fills with blood, and that's exactly what it's designed to do.

I've included some illustrations here to show you that penises can look so different from one person to the next, both when they're flaccid or when they're erect. These are all normal.

Normal penises are different in appearance, shape, length, skin colour and thickness. Your penis is covered with loose fitting skin that is usually a little more darkly coloured than the rest of your body. An erect penis may be pretty straight, or curved sideways or downwards. Some penises are **circumcised** and some are not. If you have loose skin over the head of your penis (called the **foreskin**) then you are not circumcised. If the loose skin of your penis, when it is limp, comes to just over the start of the head of your penis, you are circumcised.

WORDS FOR PENIS
WILLY, DICK, PRICK, JOHNSON, PERCY,
JOHN THOMAS, COCK, OLD FELLA, STIFFY,
TROUSERSNAKE, SNAKE, PISSPUMP, PETER,
FIREHOSE, HOT ROD, SAUSAGE, SHLONG,
WOODY, THINGY, JOYSTICK.

UNCIRCUMCISED

CIRCUMCISED

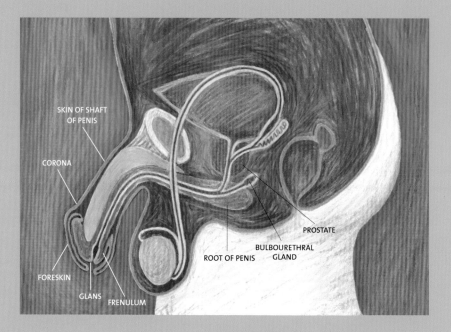

SKIN OF SHAFT
OF PENIS

CORONA

PROSTATE

BULBOURETHRAL
GLAND

ROOT OF PENIS

FORESKIN

GLANS

FRENULUM

If boys are circumcised it is usually a few days after birth, although it can be, and is, done later in life. Circumcision is done by cutting the foreskin away so that the head of the penis is exposed. This makes it easier to clean the **glans**—that's the head—than if the skin covers it. If you are uncircumcised, you need to pull back the foreskin to expose the glans to clean it. Occasionally a boy is born with a foreskin that is too tight so it can't be pulled back, but this can be effectively treated by a doctor.

Your penis contains the spongy urethra that deals with urine and semen. The urethra in your penis works in a special way. When it is not being used by urine or semen it collapses flat so that it doesn't leak. It can do this because it's not really a tube. The urethra opens only when there is enough fluid pressure from muscle contractions in the system.

The **corona** is the ridge on the head of the penis where it meets the shaft. And the **frenulum** attaches the skin of the shaft to the head of the penis. Especially around that place, your penis is loaded with touch receptors and nerves, making it very sensitive to touch.

Prostate—that's not prostrate!

The **prostate** (that's not prostrate, which means lying flat out like a lizard!) is a gland about the size of a walnut. It lies just under the bladder. When the prostate wall muscles contract, it expels the thin milky secretions of the gland and does its part to give **umph** to spurt out the semen. The secretions help the sperm swim and it protects the sperm when they get into the acidic environment of the female vagina.

When we get aroused and the body thinks we are going to ejaculate, the **bulbourethral glands** automatically release a mucous (known as pre-cum) that washes away any urine and lines the walls of the urethra so that the sperm have a trouble-free run to the finishing line. The pre-cum has another function too, it's nice and slippery, so when it leaks out the hole in the end of the erect penis it lubricates the penis in preparation for penetration of a vagina. It's a clear liquid, but beware it may contain sperm and any sperm may cause a pregnancy if it gets near a woman's egg.

WORDS FOR ERECTIONS
STIFFY, WOODY, BAR, BONER,
HARD ON, POP-UP, CHUBBY

Erections ... on the bus ... and for no apparent reason

Boys get erections from the time they are babies. At puberty your erections become more common and you will notice them more. Your penis is designed to become erect when you are sexually aroused, so that it can be inserted into the female vagina during sex and deliver sperm. The penis needs to be stiff, or erect, to be able to push into the vagina and ejaculate.

I was maybe around 9 or 10 years old. One kid brought in a black and white photo of an erect penis, and we couldn't figure out which way was up in the photo. Heated debate there.

If I get one and I don't want it, I think about the most non-sexual thing I possibly can, so disgusting it turns me off, like a filthy dog, and next minute it's gone.

I never want an erection when I'm wearing only boxers or undies cause it looks bigger than it really is, bigger than if I have jeans on.

37

But how does it work?

Well, inside your penis there are three columns of spongy tissue, like cylinders. Even though an erection is sometimes called a 'boner', there is no bone in the penis, instead erections are all about blood flow.

When we get sexually aroused the brain sends a signal to release a chemical to make more blood flow into the penis. The system works like a pump: blood gets pumped into the penis and fills the cylinders inside. These cylinders are like sponges so as they fill up, they expand to grow bigger and bigger. At the same time the expanded cylinders flatten the veins that let the blood out. This traps the blood and stops it running away, so the penis grows bigger, stiffer and harder, a bit like pumping up a bike tyre with air—the more you pump in the harder it gets. That's why an erection is sometimes called a 'hard on'.

If you unscrew a bicycle valve, down comes the air pressure, down goes the tyre. Likewise, when the cylinders damming the blood in the penis go down, they let the blood flow out again, so down goes the erect penis. This happens naturally after we come or ejaculate. If we are anxious, worried or our attention wanders it can make the erection go down too.

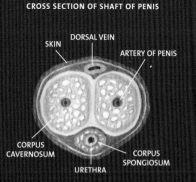

CROSS SECTION OF SHAFT OF PENIS

SKIN
DORSAL VEIN
ARTERY OF PENIS
CORPUS CAVERNOSUM
CORPUS SPONGIOSUM
URETHRA

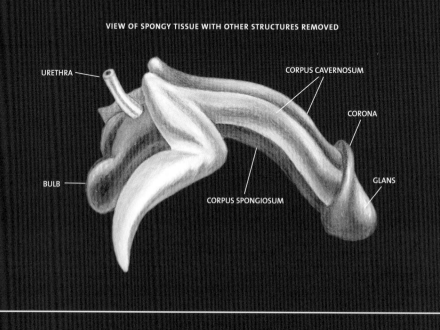

VIEW OF SPONGY TISSUE WITH OTHER STRUCTURES REMOVED

URETHRA
CORPUS CAVERNOSUM
CORONA
BULB
CORPUS SPONGIOSUM
GLANS

What do you mean it can happen any time?

At puberty, boys start getting **spontaneous erections**. They can happen for no apparent reason at all, like when we are bored in class, and sometimes when we least want them to happen. Erections can happen without us deciding to have an erection, the body just does its thing.

It can be sooo embarrassing to have an erection in public. They can come at tricky times, like when you're talking to a girl or sitting on the bus next to a woman. Most people won't even notice if you don't draw their attention to it. **So pull your jumper down or hold something over it**.

It is quite normal not to be able to get an erection sometimes, especially if you are anxious. It doesn't mean there is necessarily a physical problem if this happens occasionally. **It's normal.**

Erections can also happen when we have sexy thoughts, play with our penis, see something sexy, imagine or fantasise, or from a smell or something we hear. Sometimes we get an erection because we have a full bladder which affects the erection nerves. You can't have a pee with a full erection though, it has to go down a bit first.

 **I can remember an almost daily event, I'd be sitting on the bus coming home from school and the gentle rocking and vibration of the bus would give me an erection. It didn't matter if I didn't want one, my penis had then (and still sometimes has now) a mind of its own (as you may already know!). Up it would come making a huge tent of my school trousers, it seemed to me as if everyone on the bus must surely notice. It was even worse if there was a woman sitting next to me on the bus, in which case I desperately tried to hide it by putting my school bag on my lap. Then the trick was holding the bag in front of me when getting out of the bus. Walking rapidly away from the bus stop near home usually brought things under control before I got home.**

Did you know ...

It is usual to have about three or four erections in your sleep at night. You may not even be aware of it happening. Having these erections is the body's way of keeping the tissues in the penis healthy by regularly flooding them with nutritious blood. These night erections just come up and go down, and may not involve ejaculation.

Some people might get a sensation, but before you hit puberty you don't really know what it feels like when you ejaculate. You hear all these stories of like ... that's cum, YUK! But you don't know what it looks like until it's happened to you, you don't go 'Oh hey, can I have a look?'

Ejaculation

Ejaculation can only happen when the penis is erect. It can be fully or nearly fully erect. Ejaculation is also called 'coming'. It usually happens after continuously rubbing the penis, especially the glans and frenulum area, for example, when we play with it using our hand or during sex. The sensations build up until we come or orgasm. A hard erect penis can't stay that way indefinitely. It will in time become soft again even without ejaculation.

The first time can be a real surprise!

Our first ejaculation can take us by surprise. Often our first ejaculation happens when we are asleep and that's called a **wet dream**. I'll talk about wet dreams on the next page. I'll also talk about **masturbation**. This is when we play with our penis until we ejaculate.

On average, young men will be able to first ejaculate when they're about 13 ½ years old, but at this stage there might not be enough sperm to fertilise an egg. This will probably take about 6–18 months from the first time you ejaculate. Of course it may occur earlier too.

Most boys never tell anyone, not their parents or friends, about first ejaculations, but many joke about it. The secrecy is usually because, somehow, we get an unfortunate and incorrect message that ejaculation is a secret, shameful thing, linked to masturbation, and not really OK. **Ejaculation is very normal and nothing to be ashamed about. It happens to all boys and men.**

In fact, talking about ejaculation with people you trust is important because it helps you to know that it is a healthy, normal, natural part of life.

I can remember being really surprised, in the early stages of masturbating, that when I ejaculated I felt so amazingly weak. I was very fit, could run cross-country and wouldn't be tired. But ejaculation, I can remember the tiredness and my strength going, almost dizziness.

Wet dreams

Possums are nocturnal animals, which means they are active at night and sleep during the day. Erections are a bit like possums because they also love to come out at night when you are in bed and even when you are asleep. When erections happen at night when you are asleep and you ejaculate or 'come', this is called a **nocturnal emission**, which sounds like something the army does at night!

But the everyday word for it is **wet dream**. All young men have them. It is a natural way to release the semen and sperm that are being produced. Wet dreams might involve sexually exciting dreams, but then again they might not. In either case, we may wake up to find we have an erection and are experiencing highly pleasurable feelings in the penis and then we ejaculate, or we may wake up just after we ejaculate, or not wake up at all. This happens without even touching your penis with your hand, it all happens on autopilot!

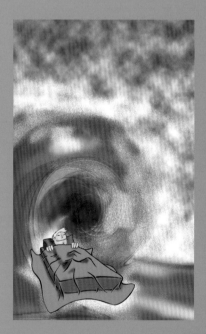

Wet dreams are nothing to be embarrassed about, although when it first happens it can be confusing or scary.

Sometimes you might wake up at the end of a wet dream just as you've ejaculated or shortly after, to find the semen on your pyjamas, sheets or the skin of your belly and penis. Your first thought might be that you've wet the bed, but you haven't. Your second thought might be 'I don't want anyone to find this'. That's OK. Ejaculation is a private thing, but there is nothing to be ashamed of. It is totally normal.

We soon get used to wet dreams—we might even look forward to having them. Wet dreams continue to happen regularly into adulthood, and for some men well beyond middle age.

When I woke up at the end of my first wet dream, I looked down to find all this white sticky stuff all over my pyjamas and my belly. I thought I had sprung a leak and had no idea what it was. I actually thought my penis was broken. I was worried so I went to tell my mother. She was very calm and reassured me that nothing was wrong and put me back to bed.

From playing Power Ranger to playing with yourself ... masturbation

Boys and girls naturally touch their genitals from the time they are babies. Touching our sex organs for pleasure is called **masturbation** (MASS-TER-BAY-SHON) and it is a completely natural thing to do. During puberty masturbation changes from childlike fiddling to rubbing the penis to give ourselves pleasure.

Masturbation can start with your penis limp, or it may already be erect ... and it usually ends with ejaculation (coming). But it may not go that far, it may be only pleasant touching of yourself. Most men masturbate from puberty, through adult life, including at times while in a sexual relationship.

Masturbation is sometimes called a hand job. Our hands have more nerve endings than our genitals, nevertheless the exciting feelings when we masturbate do not come from our fingers! Some say that if you sit on your hand till it goes numb, that it feels like someone else's hand!

Ants love semen! I used to slop up the semen with a handkerchief and then just drop them down the side of the bed and eventually they would get eaten by ants! They'd end up full of holes because the ants had eaten holes in them. That was very mortifying because then I had to dispose of the handkerchiefs. You know I can't remember how I did that. My mum never mentioned it to me.

It will make you go blind ... no it won't!

There are lots of masturbation myths ... you'll go blind, hairs will grow on your palms, you'll go crazy, it causes acne, you'll go bald ... none of these are true, thank heavens!

In the old days—like way before you were born—masturbation was frowned upon. Science was not as advanced and it was thought that sperm contained all of life, without needing an egg from a woman. So it was thought that wasting sperm was wasting life. Now that we have better science we know differently. In some cultures sperm is still regarded as vital energy that should be preserved. Religion and culture

I can remember really vividly my first ejaculation because I must have been lying in bed masturbating. I remember ejaculating and I was shocked that something had happened. I thought I must be bleeding, I turned the light on and looked down and there was this white stuff. I had no idea what it was, or what it was about, but I was really relieved that it wasn't blood.

I used to have a problem with what to do with the semen after it came out. One day I realised that semen dries pretty much invisibly on light colours and becomes a sort of powder. I rolled over to the edge of the bed and the semen went onto the carpet beside my bed. That turned out to be the perfect solution for me. Eventually so much of it went down there that a mark appeared, but Mum never mentioned it. The tricky bit was getting my timing right to roll over at just the right time and hoping Mum never walked in soon after in bare feet.

I had just discovered masturbation and my penis was getting sore from the friction, so I decided to check out the bathroom cupboard for good lubricants. Each day I experimented with another tube or bottle of stuff in the cupboard that might be good and slippery ... Mum's hand creams, toothpaste (not good!), moisturisers, sorbolene, Vaseline, sunburn cream— I tried the lot! Eventually I had a go with Dad's aftershave ... well it took me about two weeks to go back to the cupboard ... it stung like mad!

play a role too and that's why today some people are still taught that masturbation is sinful or wrong, and why so many people are afraid to admit that they do it or feel guilty or ashamed when they do it.

Other people believe masturbation is OK and healthy. **It's definitely, definitely, normal.** But depending on what your family believes, what religion you are and what your cultural practices are, you might have been taught different things about masturbation. **The important thing to remember here is that, you got it, we're all different and we're all entitled to believe different things.** People have different opinions. You will need to make up your own mind, because it is your body, your choice. That's what becoming a man brings, responsibility to make up your own mind.

It's a private thing

But if you're cool about the whole masturbation thing, you need to remember that it's not a public act to be done out on the footpath! It is something done in a private place because it is a personal thing. I have never heard of someone masturbating in bed in the morning and then rushing into the kitchen saying, 'Hey Mum, I just had a fantastic jerk off, now what's for breakfast?' That doesn't mean you can't talk to anyone about it. In fact, if you can talk to a brother or cousin or an adult you trust and feel safe with, you should. Remember, they have almost certainly done it too.

Masturbation—can it hurt?

Masturbation is not physically harmful, but like anything else in life, if you over practise to extremes, you might become addicted. Definitely not a healthy thing to do. The other thing that might happen is a physical problem. If you rub your penis for too long or too often without lubrication, then the skin (of the penis, not the hand!) can chafe and get really sore. You can avoid this by using a lubricant like soap, or a cream.

Take your time

Many Puberty Boys masturbate in secret and do it in a hurry so they won't be caught. So this means they may be **anxious** when they masturbate. If we masturbate too often in a hurried way, in other words, trying to come as soon as possible, or we get used to always being anxious about being discovered, this can lead to anxieties later in life. So **if you are going to masturbate, do it when you can take your time, relax and do it in a private place that is anxiety free.**

About penis size

Puberty Boys, as you become sexually aware you'll naturally start to notice and compare your penis to others. Trust me, it'll happen. Judging by all the guys who have spoken to me about it, there is a word for people who have never worried about the size of their penis ... 'girls'.

Your penis, like everything else about you, is unique and made just for you. This means that if you and your friends dropped your daks and compared with each other, you'll see that every single one of you is different. We inherit our penis size just like our hair colour or height. So there is absolutely no good reason to compare yourself with others and worry about your size—you're perfect just the way you are!

But OK, OK, you still want to talk about size? I'll give you some facts.

On average, the erect penis in a white Caucasian adult is 15 cm (6 inches) long (measured along the top!) and 3.5 cm (1 3/8 inches) in diameter (that's across, not around!). Anatomy books, doctors, experts and sex researchers all confirm this. Most erect penises vary between 10 cm (4 inches) and 20 cm (8 inches) long, but the vast bulk, 75–90 per cent of penises, are between 13 cm (5 inches) and 18 cm (7 inches). Average penis length may be longer or shorter in non-Caucasian races.

WORDS FOR MASTURBATION
WANK, BEAT THE MEAT, JERK OFF, PUMP, SPANK THE MONKEY, CHOKE THE CHICKEN, WHACK OFF, PULL OFF, HAND JOB, BEAT OFF, SPIT-SHINING THE OLD WATER PUMP, WAXING THE BRASS CANDLESTICK, PLAYING CARDS WITH ONLY ONE HAND ON THE TABLE, RIDING THE QUARTER-HORSE, GIVING IN TO THE HAND POLICE

I was about 15, in the bathroom with the door closed. I was pulling myself off, standing at the bathroom basin with my erection covered in soap suds. Suddenly the door opened, my grandfather walked in, his eyes widened as he saw what I was doing, but cool as a cat he turned around and said, 'Sorry I thought you were cleaning your teeth!' He never mentioned it to anyone.

It's all in the way you look at it!

I can remember myself at puberty having worries about whether mine was big enough (I would sometimes cheat and measure along the bottom side which is longer!). I made a few mistakes in my thinking that didn't help at all.

Trap No. 1: I didn't realise that size differences when limp can be misleading. We usually see other penises when they are not erect, like in the showers or change room. There is often a greater difference between limp penises than the same ones when erect, so a penis which looks much smaller limp, may turn out to be much similar in size to the ones that look larger, when erect. It is not always possible to predict the size of an erect penis by looking at it limp, especially if it's a cold day when shrinkage happens! Although stretching a non-erect penis to its extreme gives the erect length when it fills with blood. A doctor friend of mine, a men's sexual health specialist, told me: 'It is not always possible to guess an erect length from looking at a flaccid [soft] penis but generally the larger flaccid penises don't need much guessing. The smaller ones can be the big surprise!'

Trap No. 2: I also made the mistake of comparing my penis to penises in erotic magazines. Men in these magazines are chosen precisely because they have a large penis that is **NOT** the normal or average penis size.

Trap No. 3: I fell for another trap too. To illustrate, take something like a pen, about the length of a penis, hold it up so you see it square on. Notice how long it looks? Now hold it down where your penis is, like a limp penis and tilt it downwards. Notice how it looks shorter? I used to look down on my penis without realising it looks shorter from that angle than from another person's view, and I saw theirs as longer than they did!

Puberty Boys often worry, 'Is it big enough?' As one woman said to me, perhaps the more important question is, 'How can I give and receive pleasure with what I've got? What it boils down to is that it's not the size of the boat, but the motion of the ocean that matters.'

Puberty Boys, remember, we are who we are, and we are pretty special. We all need to accept and love ourselves for who we are. How we treat and love the people around us has little to do with our body or how we look. It has to do with our character, what is in our heart and our ability to love and be loved. Loving someone, and being loved, has more to do with the size of your brain and heart than the size of your penis.

Q&A

I've heard a penis called a boner, does it have a bone in it?

Some mammals have a bone in their penis, but not humans. When an erection occurs the penis gets stiff and hard just like it does have a bone in it.

Is it true that as you get older you look more like you've been circumcised?

No, that's not true. If we have a foreskin then no matter what age we are it will pretty much cover the head of the penis when it is not erect. However if we have an erection, the foreskin is pulled back as the penis grows longer and then it can be hard to tell if someone is circumcised or not, but has nothing to do with age.

Sometimes after I ejaculate when I next take a leak it sprays all over the place like a garden sprinkler. What's happening?

Yep, that happens. A bit of semen dries in the opening at the end of the penis so the flow of urine goes crazy when it hits. It usually stops as the sperm is washed away or you might have to stop urinating (can be tricky!), clear the hole with a rub of your finger, and have another go.

I get distracted standing there peeing into the toilet bowl, I sometimes miss and wet the bowl or the floor. Mum gets sick of it. What can I do?

It's all about concentration. To improve in this department try putting an imaginary tennis ball in the bowl and aim for that, it really improves hand–penis coordination.

Privacy Puberty is a time when we start to need time alone with our body, to dress ourselves, to look at it closely, take care of it, explore it and get to know it in more detail. We are entitled to private time alone to do these things. It is OK to ask your parents or others in the house for privacy at these times. You may choose to close the door to your bedroom or private space when you want to be alone. It is OK to ask that if your bedroom door is closed that people knock before they come in and wait till you ask them to come in. If you start to respect others' rights and privacy needs, like not running straight into your parents' bedroom without knocking, then others will respect your privacy too. **The more respect you give to others the more you will get back.**

Chapter 5

GIRLS

are changing too

There are some things you'll need to know about girls' bodies as you read *Puberty Boy*. Boys have a penis, girls have a vagina. Duh! I hear you say, I already knew that!

In this book you are reading about the reasons why our bodies change and what they're getting ready for. So when I talk about girls, I mention things like the:

◎ **Vagina:** which is the female sex organ down there between a girl's legs. It's the passage the penis goes into during sex to deliver sperm so that they can swim up to fertilise the waiting egg.

◎ **Ovaries:** which are the two production areas (or factories) inside the female pelvis that store and mature eggs. At puberty ovaries start to **ovulate**, or send a new egg into the **fallopian tubes** each month. If that egg meets and joins with a sperm, the woman becomes pregnant with a baby.

◎ **Uterus:** or womb, is where a fertilised egg or foetus grows during pregnancy.

◎ **Clitoris:** which is about the size of a pea, and is a girl's sexual pleasure spot.

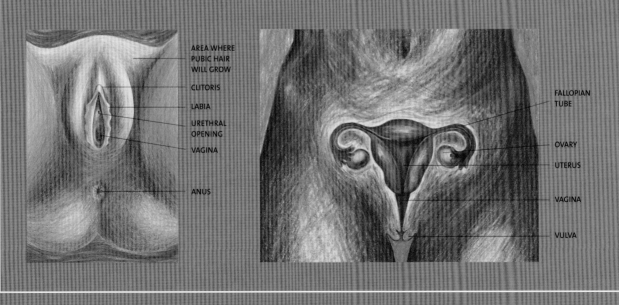

AREA WHERE PUBIC HAIR WILL GROW

CLITORIS

LABIA

URETHRAL OPENING

VAGINA

ANUS

FALLOPIAN TUBE

OVARY

UTERUS

VAGINA

VULVA

◎ **Periods:** which are also called the monthly **menstrual cycle** or **menstruation**. Each month, if the waiting egg is not fertilised, it goes out of a girl's body through her vagina along with the womb lining and some blood. This is also known as 'that time of the month' and lots of other names too. A girl needs to wear tampons or sanitary pads to absorb the blood that comes out of her vagina. The bleeding lasts 3–7 days.

What happens to girls during puberty?
Girls go through puberty as well and plenty of stuff happens to them.

◎ They get their periods (menstrual bleeding).
◎ They can be 'premenstrual', emotional and moody just before they get their periods.
◎ Their bodies change: they grow breasts, they grow taller and they start getting curves all over their body.
◎ They grow pubic hair and underarm hair.
◎ They may get pimples and acne.
◎ They may get confused and worried about all the changes going on as well!

Eastro what? A girl's hormone you say?

From the time we're babies, boys and girls are taught to behave in different ways according to their gender. At puberty, a boy's body is flooded with testosterone, while a girl's body gets **oestrogen** (pronounced EAST-RO-JEN). This is the main female hormone. Boys have oestrogen too, just like girls have testosterone. But boys have more testosterone and girls have more oestrogen.

Most girls become more socially active and communicative—they can easily relate to other people. Boys tend to be thing and action oriented, whereas girls are more relationship oriented. So there's a lot more going on than just physical changes between boys and girls at puberty.

Puberty Boys are usually 1–2 years behind girls in the hormone rush of puberty. You might feel that girls your own age or a little older are suddenly from another planet. Or you might be very comfortable and confident that you know exactly what they're thinking, especially if you have older sisters in the house.

Chapter 6

You are
IN CHARGE
of your own body!

What does 'I'm in charge of my body' mean? It means you have the right and power to say what happens to it, in it, and around it, especially when it comes to other people touching you in any sexual way. That means that you have the right to, and should, say a big loud 'No' to anyone who touches you in a way that is sexual, or that you don't want to happen, no matter who they are, how powerful they are, or what they promise they will do, or won't do, for you. This applies even to relatives or people you know well. Saying 'NO' or 'STOP' is the start to keeping yourself safe.

What is unwanted touching?

An unwanted touch or action is one that **YOU** decide is not welcome. Such as when any other person, male or female, touches you, massages, strokes, kisses you, acts sexually, speaks sexually, exposes themselves, or asks (or tries to force or trick) you to touch them in any way that is sexual. That applies to any part of your body, or theirs, especially genitals. This applies to people you might meet on the Internet too. If they ask for your personal details like where you live, or they send you rude pictures, then end your contact with them and tell your parents.

Non-sexual touching is OK and healthy with people you know, provided you want it and it feels OK to you. Non-sexual touch is something like a hug. Trust your feelings about any touching that goes too far.

What can I do if unwanted touching happens?

◎ If you get a feeling that unwanted touching is going to happen, or it starts to happen to you, the first thing to do is to say 'NO' or 'STOP' loudly.
◎ Walk or run away immediately to a safe person or place.
◎ Don't keep it a secret! Tell an adult you trust as soon as you can. This can be a parent, teacher, grandparent, uncle or aunt, older brother or sister, mentor, or someone you trust.

If you want to talk to someone outside your safety network, you can call the Kids Helpline. They're available 24 hours a day and they have trained people who talk to kids every day. Their number is 1800 551 800.

Chapter 7

Becoming aware of
SEXUALITY

During puberty, you might find that suddenly, you start thinking about and seeing yourself not as a boy, but as a young man. You might become aware that your body is getting ready for sexual maturity, and you might start to notice the differences between yourself and girls. You might even find that the girl who got on your nerves just last week is somehow making your heart beat faster and you want to hang around her more often!

These changes that happen on the inside are to do with the growing sexuality of you and your peers, girls and boys. Inside us, we naturally become more aware of sexy feelings, and of others' sexuality. A look from someone, a touch or the sight or thought of someone (of either sex) can get your blood racing and thoughts excited. I'm sure you've noticed how many images there are of women's bodies on TV, in movies, magazines and on advertising billboards. The change that happens during puberty is that you'll start to notice girls' bodies and they might make you think about sex. This is what's called a sexual response and it's perfectly normal. On the other hand, if you don't have sexy feelings, that's normal too. They'll come later when you are ready.

If you think you're becoming interested sexually in girls, this is completely normal and natural. But—**and a big BUT here**—becoming more sexual with yourself is one thing, having sex with other people is a lot more complex. There is a lot to learn about yourself first before you can start having sex with other people. This is a very adult thing to do.

As puberty unfolds there may be pressure all around, mates and media, to have sex. As you grow older there will be many decisions you have to make about your sexuality and relationships. Your body may sometimes feel ready, but at puberty the rest of you will be a long way from ready to have sex with others. That's where responsibility, respect and awareness can help you make good decisions.

You see a lot of movies about positions and stuff and you wonder about that, the way it goes into the vagina, and you find yourself, for experience, doing the movements. I'm being serious!

I found out what sex was when my friend opened up a book randomly to a page and read it out.

Finding out about sex

Having awareness and knowledge about sex means that you are in transition from being a boy to being a young man. Being respectful and responsible with the knowledge is one of your challenges.

Hey, how did you find out?

Boys find out about sex in all sorts of ways, some by accident, some are educated by their parents, some from school lessons, movies or the media. For some it comes as a total surprise, for others they already know a bit about it. There's no right or wrong way, we all learn about it differently. Some parents and some boys find it difficult to talk about sexuality and some find it easy. Religions and cultures also influence what is OK to talk about.

When are you ready for sex?

Because this is a book about puberty, I'm giving you some information you need to know now, but not everything about sex. Just because you know about sex does not make you have sex earlier, and doesn't mean you can, or will, start to have sex now.

The average age for first sex in young men is about 17. But there's no rule that says you have to start having sex at a certain age. Every one of us needs to make this decision according to what we feel, what we believe and if we're ready. There are some teenagers who start having sex early, say around age 14. If you think that 14 isn't emotionally mature enough to handle it, many of these early starters would say you're right. It's been published that boys who started having sex at an early age made comments like, 'The whole thing was confusing, I didn't realise. I want things to go back to the way things were before we did it'.

I'm not going to give you a lecture about sex. This is something for you to decide about. The best way for you to ensure you don't make a bad

Did you know ...

There's a difference between having sex and making love, and between ejaculation and orgasm. Each is linked with the other, but they're different things. Sex is just the physical act, just like ejaculation is a physical release. Making love involves sex plus deep loving feelings between two people, and orgasm is a physical, emotional and sometimes spiritual experience that is the pleasure peak of making love with someone we care about. It takes a lot of maturity for this to happen.

decision and do something you regret is to carefully think about and decide what you want, and why you want it, before doing anything. Then carry that as a strong, clear intention and stick to it. Self-control is the way a strong man makes sure he does what he decides to do.

Sometimes guys think that sex is a scoring competition with their mates, especially when it comes to losing their **virginity**. They do it because they hope that having sex and talking about it will improve their reputation and status with their crowd. But this only makes them look like they're bragging or that they're making it up, and ends up undermining their confidence.

We had a sex education class at school and it was in the evening. I couldn't figure out a way to tell my mother there was a sex education class ... so I arranged for my friends to come by my place to pick me up. My friends rolled up and she asked one of them what it was about and he didn't have any problem saying, 'It's a sex education night'. Straightaway my mother said, 'Well you're not going' ... so it was very embarrassing for me in front of my mates to be staying at home.

I was about 12, and I went along to a 'father and son night', and he sat in the front with all the other dads, I sat in the back with all the other kids. They put up all these slides of penises and what intercourse was about. I was just completely astonished, I had absolutely no idea it was about that at all. It had never occurred to me that it would be about reproduction. I thought about it for weeks afterwards, I was so blown away by it.

How do you tell if you're gay?

Throughout history in all cultures a small percentage of people have been attracted to people of the same sex—that is boy likes boy, girl likes girl. **Heterosexuals** are attracted to people of the other sex—girl/boy. When **homosexual** men are attracted to other men, that's what's known as being **gay**. Homosexual women are called **lesbians**. **Bisexual** people are attracted to both sexes. Research suggests that between 5 and 15 per cent of men are gay.

Gay men don't know why they are attracted to men, they just are. When gay men open up about being gay; it is called 'coming out', but gay men don't just wake up one morning, realise they are gay, and come out.

In my mid-teens I realised there was something different about my sexuality, although I didn't know what to do with that at the time. I remember having some thoughts about being with other guys, but not really well formed in any way. I didn't know what being gay was. Now, much later, I've come out.

My childhood was very painful and confusing. I was picked on for my gentle nature and belittled for the most wonderful part of me, my playful, tender, affectionate self. By the time puberty hit, I had got a real message that I had a choice between two paths. I could be John Wayne and shut down my tender loving feelings, not only towards my male friends, but even towards my female friends who I must now start 'making'. Or I could be queer, which I was not.

There is usually a time of feeling different, not being sure and experimentation. This is different to exploring your sexuality with another boy, which doesn't make you gay. It just helps discover feelings.

Fear of gays and of being gay

Some people are frightened of being gay and misguidedly hate gays because they actually hate those feelings, or the possibility of those feelings, in themselves. This is what's called **homophobia** and it's about fear, and often hatred, of gay people, usually based on prejudice and not actually knowing someone who is gay. It's like fear of the dark—we're frightened of what might be out there.

It's common to be aroused sometimes by seeing someone's penis or by being in a certain setting, like the change room. It's also common for boys to fantasise about other boys, even to experiment with masturbating together, the way girls might practise kissing at sleepovers. But tests prove that physical touching does not make you gay. Being gay is about feeling a certain sexual, emotional, sometimes spiritual way towards other men. It's about having a different way of seeing ourselves and other gay people. Gay men are often more in touch than other men with the feminine side of the human nature we all share. These qualities are fundamental to how gay people are made up inside, you don't catch it like a cold or make yourself gay.

If you're not macho and you cry, does that mean you're gay?

To make sure they are not labelled as gay, or make sure they are 'manly' or tough, Puberty Boys can go too far the other way and put away the playful, tender and affectionate parts of themselves, especially with other males. So they hardly touch each other at all—no hugs and definitely no tears. They barely shake hands and maybe punch each other or wrestle when they're mucking around.

When we repress our feelings like this we often find it hard to ever get them back, even with girls. As guys and men, we need to remember that showing affection for each other is very manly. There is nothing wrong with it.

Puberty Boys, ask yourselves: what's wrong with showing affection for people we care about? Nothing! So don't deprive yourself of the love of your friends just because of an idea of what being tough or macho is.

I was straight for most of my life, marriage, two children, mortgage, mates etc. But I had to find my way because I just simply couldn't fit into the mould. After years of trying to 'fix' myself, coming out was something I had to do.

Ask questions ... communicate

Lots of Puberty Boys aged between 10 and 14 years ask questions about sex and body changes. They have questions like, 'If I shave my legs does that mean I'm gay?' (it doesn't necessarily), and issues like being bullied, coming out about being gay to parents, rejection by friends and what to do. If you are confused, or need to talk about some problems, or do feel you are gay and need support dealing with your decision, your family, discrimination or anything else, there are many people you can talk to, like:

- ◎ **Mum, Dad, and your safety network:** I encourage you to try talking to your mum and dad about problems. But I understand that sometimes you feel you can't. If that's the case, then try your older brother or sister or cousin or someone in your safety network, or a person you trust.
- ◎ **Ring a counsellor:** If you want to talk to a counsellor on the phone, the Kids Helpline is available 24 hours a day and it's a free call. Their number is: 1800 551 800.

There was the Under 14s footy carnival coming up and I was playing in it. I'd arranged with my parents to stay the night at a friend's so we can get the bus early the next day to the carnival. Eventually we laid down in bed to go to sleep and he asks me if I can make sperm, and I say 'nuh' and he says 'you want to look?' and I said 'oh, yeah', so we both are whacking off and he makes this sperm which blows me out. We got beaten in the footy next day, I think it had something to do with the fact that we were both tired. Neither of us turned out gay!

Q&A

When you're aroused in any way and you get an erection, and if you like, keep going, will you always ejaculate?

No, you can keep going till you come, but if you stop stimulating yourself before you go too far, the erection will go down without ejaculation, and this will cause you no harm.

Do we all grow up and just want to masturbate?

Nearly all teenagers masturbate, most do it frequently, a few wait until they are 20 or so to start. I've asked heaps of adult men of all ages about whether they still masturbate. I've only ever met one man who said he has never masturbated and that was for religious reasons. The rest have all said they are still masturbating (some do it more often than others) as adults, and men continue to do so even if they are in a relationship and having regular sex, so it's quite usual.

Can girls masturbate?

Yep, girls and women masturbate.

I've heard of premature ejaculation but I don't know what it is.

Premature ejaculation is coming before you want to. For some people this is 30 seconds and for others 20 minutes. It's not so much about how long it takes to come, it's more about whether that time works. If it works for everyone, it's not premature.

I've heard of blue balls, is this real?

Yep, these are sometimes called lover's balls too. This is a deep uncomfortable ache that feels like it's in your balls. It can happen if you have been kissing and cuddling with someone for hours, or aroused for a long period. Your scrotum goes bluish because of all the blood that is pumped into that area when you are excited. The ache is because of the increased fluid waiting to be expelled. The ache will go away without any harm.

If you masturbate do your palms get hairy?

Well violinists who continually rub their instruments on their neck can end up with a rough hairy patch there. But no, you don't go hairy, or bald or blind!

Chapter 8

Staying healthy ... it's about ATTITUDE!

Body odour (BO) has a deadly enemy ... soap!

Perspiration, or sweat, is your body's way of keeping you cool. Sweat itself doesn't smell, but bacteria thrives in it and releases natural, but rather unpleasant smells, especially to others! During puberty your sweat glands are more active, sometimes overactive, and they can bring smells to armpits, feet and genitals. Daily showering (more often if you're always playing sport and sweating heavily) and washing your whole body, especially genitals, feet and armpits, is the way to keep BO at bay (singing in the shower while having a half-hearted quick rinse without soap won't cut it!). If you have sensitive skin, soap may cause irritation, so use a very mild soap or body wash.

Yesterday's clothes ... yesterday's sweat

Yesterday's clothes have yesterday's sweat (and worse!) on them. Do you ever smell your clothes before putting them on? It's a good idea. Trust your nose to tell you when clothes are dirty and need to be washed, especially in the armpit and genital department. Change your socks and underwear every day, and if you exercise, change your clothes after sweating in them. Natural fibre clothes (like cotton or wool) breathe best.

What's the difference between deodorant and anti-perspirant?

Deodorants are like perfume. They cover up a smell (they're not always successful!) but they don't stop you from sweating. Anti-perspirants actually try to stop or dry up the sweat. But take note, anti-perspirants contain aluminium, which might be harmful to the body if used a lot and over a long time. Talk to your dad or brother about some options here, especially about what works for them.

When the hairs on my thighs were starting to grow, I already had hairs down below, there were black dots coming up on my legs and there was all this talk about blackheads going around. So I spent a couple of hours in the bath scrubbing them out, scrubbing my legs red raw and it turns out they were hairs ... I actually scrubbed out the hair follicles, and even now the hair is patchy or has grown a bit weird on my thighs! So it's OK to have black dots on your thighs ... let 'em grow!

Pimples and acne

Oh no, I hear you say, on top of everything I need to worry about pimples? Unfortunately, for some of us, pimples are part of puberty. But the good news is that there are many ways to treat pimples so the whole experience doesn't have to be painful and you won't have to live with your head in a paper bag for years!

What is acne?

Acne and pimples are different. Pimples are the small or large lumps you get on your skin, and acne is an inflammation of the sebaceous gland; it's more severe and it can cause scarring.

Our skin produces sebum, an oily substance that is made by the sebaceous glands near the root of each hair growing in our skin. Sebum helps keep skin moist and maintain a healthy population of bacteria on the skin's surface. As you might know already, not all bacteria is bad bacteria.

Where does acne come from?

Acne is not caused by dirty skin pores, so scrap that idea. It's not caused by junk food either! Studies have found no connection between acne or chocolate or chips or pizza.

What happens is that during puberty, the skin produces more sebum than before because there's a big surge of hormone production, so the cells of the hair follicles get stickier and they block the skin's pores so the sebum can't get out. If the blockage happens under the skin, you get a **whitehead**, but if the blockage reaches the air it turns dark and becomes a **blackhead**.

Sometimes acne bacteria get into the tissue around the blackhead or whitehead and it becomes inflamed. That's when you can get small red bumps, white or yellow pus-filled pimples or large red bumps.

About 90 per cent of boys (and 80 per cent of girls) get this teenage acne, some worse than others, usually starting just before puberty and sometimes lasting until they're 25. Most of this teenage acne happens on the face, upper back and chest. But you can get pimples on your stomach (it happens!) or your neck and even your bottom.

Using oil-based cosmetics can cause acne as well. Sure, that will be mostly the girls, but many guys these days use cosmetics to cover up blemishes and even out skin tones. So if you decide to use cosmetics, make sure you read the labels properly and choose ones that suit your skin type.

Some steroid medications may cause acne, and of course, genes also come into play. **If your dad or mum or brother had acne you're probably in line too.**

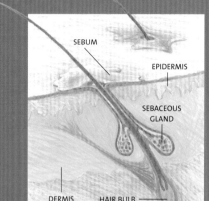

HAIR

SEBUM

EPIDERMIS

SEBACEOUS GLAND

DERMIS   HAIR BULB

HAIR FOLLICLE AND SEBACEOUS GLANDS

Pimples are really painful, it just started hurting for no reason, it got all red and bad. I used all this stuff to get rid of it that didn't work ... It went away eventually.

How can you treat pimples and acne?

You can buy over-the-counter creams at pharmacies. Treatments like creams won't get rid of pimples that are already large and red, but they can help prevent new ones. You can use creams even when your skin is looking good to prevent new pimples. Some creams claim they can make a difference straightaway but most treatments usually take up to six weeks. So don't give up too soon, keep trying till you know for sure it's not working. Because everyone's skin is different, you might have to try a few treatments before you find one that works for you.

If you decide to try out a treatment from a pharmacy, you'll find staff who can guide and advise you about products that can help. They're professionals and they're trained to be sensitive to your feelings; they remember puberty too!

If over-the-counter treatment doesn't do the trick, see your doctor.

I had bad teen acne, and it wrecked my self-confidence for years after the acne had cleared. I convinced myself I was hideous to look at and there was no way anyone, male or female, would want to be close to me. Now it seems so obvious when I think of the times a girl had shown some interest and I didn't allow myself to see it. Even with friends I usually declined invitations. I didn't see how anyone could like me, since I didn't like me. I'd love to go back again and be more confident in myself, even with all the acne. Just believe in myself. That was all I really needed to do.

Step-by-step care for skin with pimples

1. The first step is to take care of yourself, and be gentle with your skin. If you rub and scrub you'll irritate the skin and make it worse.
2. Wash your face gently twice a day with water and a mild soap or cleanser, and pat it dry. Using a soap-free wash is a good idea.
3. Use oil-free skin care products.
4. If acne is on your chest or back, wear loose cotton clothing.
5. Don't squeeze or pop pimples, as it can damage the skin and cause infection and even scarring when sebum, bacteria and shed skin cells are pushed into surrounding tissue.

6. If you do have to squeeze a pimple—if one is just bursting with puss and you just can't take looking at it any longer—then wash your hands with soap and water and then very gently, using a tissue so your fingers aren't touching the pimple, slowly squeeze until it pops. Then clean it with a gentle disinfectant so the bacteria doesn't spread.

7. You can take out blackheads with a special blackhead removal tool. Yes there is such a thing! You get it from the pharmacy.

Athlete's foot—jock itch

Just when you thought you could handle all the info, I have to throw in fungus! Yes, believe it or not, fungus does grow on your skin, and athlete's foot and jock itch are both caused by fungus. They are related but different fungi. Fungi just looove to grow in warm, moist parts that don't get much fresh air—like genitals and between your toes. If you're itchy, have a rash, can smell something isn't right, or your skin is peeling or cracked, get it checked out by your doctor to confirm that it's fungus.

How do you deal with jock itch?

◎ If it turns out that you do have jock itch, the best thing to do is get a treatment and keep the area clean and dry.

◎ Don't over-wash or scrub the skin because this will cause irritation and can wash away helpful skin contents.

◎ Take special care to dry properly after showering, dabbing gently until the area is dry.

◎ Use a clean towel every day until it's gone.

◎ Expose areas to open air and sunlight as much as possible.

◎ Wash clothes often, especially a jock strap.

◎ Wear cotton clothes not polyester, because they breathe better so your skin will too.

Secrets of Puberty Boys' health

From the time we're babies, we boys are usually taught to be brave and not cry when we fall down or something hurts. We get the unfortunate message that to be a real man, we must be strong, hide our hurts, never show weakness or ask for help. So most of us end up believing this info and may not say when we're in pain or are feeling sick even when we're older.

Listen to your body—it knows what it wants!

Imagine if you were a professional footy player. If you felt a pain would you tell your coach or doctor? Of course you would, otherwise the little twinge could turn into a ripping muscle in the middle of a game! All sportspeople pay attention to their body, its whispers, wounds and illnesses, because they respect it, and they know that if they want to be fit to do what they have to do, they must care for themselves. They know that seeking help when they need it is being courageous, not weak.

A confident Puberty Boy or man is the same. He doesn't need to be macho and prove anything about himself to others. He doesn't need to take crazy risks with his body, like extreme sports, unprotected sex, smoking, or drinking too much, to prove he is a man or have friends. He is who he is, and gets respect for that. He knows puberty is the time to take more responsibility for his own health and TELL people if something is wrong.

You need to feel your balls!

Puberty Boys, if you learn how to feel your balls now, you'll be protecting yourself against testicular cancer in the future. Testicular cancer is rare, but it can happen. Feel your balls for any unusual lumps or bumps and if you suspect anything is unusual, tell your doctor straightaway.

Become familiar with the size, weight, shape, bumps and lumps on your balls **while they are healthy**. You don't have to look every day! Just check them regularly. Look out for lumps, swelling, an enlarged ball, heaviness, pain, any change in either ball, enlarged breasts or nipples, or blood or fluid building up quickly in the scrotum.

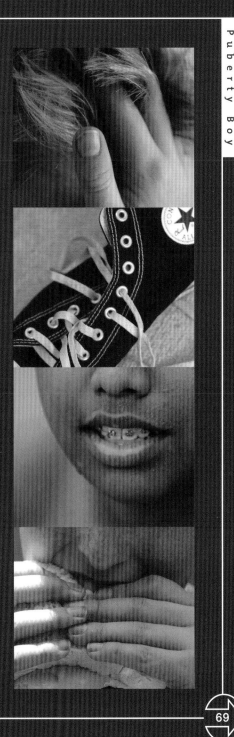

The best time to check yourself is after a hot shower when your scrotum is soft and relaxed. If you're not sure you're checking in the right way, ask your doctor about it.

STIs and safe sex

If you think you want to experiment with sex with other people, or if you've already had some experiences of this, then you need to know about **STIs**.

What are STIs?

STIs are sexually transmitted infections—as in infections you can get from other people when you have sexual contact with them. If you are mature enough to be sexual you are also old enough to take responsibility for yourself and others by staying safe.

STIs spread from one person to another through any kind of sexual activity, including if the penis touches the vagina, anus or mouth, or touching herpes or cold sores, genital warts or other people's blood. You can get STIs from kissing, especially the herpes variety, like cold sores. You can get STIs from just one contact, even the first time. You can have more than one infection at the same time; and having had one in the past does not protect you in future. And you can catch one from someone who looks very healthy. There is a heap of info on the web if you want to know more. Check out the resource list at the back of the book.

How do you protect yourself against STIs?

◎ Don't kiss or touch herpes, warts or cold sores.
◎ Always, always use a condom when having sexual activity.
◎ Avoid contact with anyone else's blood. All the big infections are transmitted through blood to blood contact.

Condoms protect everyone

Condoms are used to protect you against infections and to avoid pregnancy. Guys wear condoms on their penis so that sperm comes out in the condom only. This also protects against touching other people's skin or bodily fluids.

Some people have trouble talking about condoms, or are afraid that others will think they have an infection if they use a condom. And unfortunately, some guys don't want to use condoms because they believe they reduce sensitivity, draw attention to the penis, cause loss of erection or think it will interrupt sex.

Young men sometimes think they are invincible, that nothing can hurt them and they'll never die ... So they take risks ... this is boy thinking not young man thinking. If you care about and respect yourself, and other people, then you need to use protection. Any time you find yourself tempted to be sexual with someone without taking safety precautions like using a condom ... take a moment to decide if the thrill now is worth the risk ... worth the risk of infection later.

Chapter 9
your **BODY**
...your shape or the media shape?

Have you noticed the way guys in movies and magazines are all really good looking, have six-packs, smooth muscular chests and basically just look perfect? Sure, there are some normal looking people, even some bald ones, but they're never the main actor, they're always in the background, or sometimes they're the 'fat guy' or the 'bald guy' character who is made fun of.

If you have noticed this then you're a step ahead of the rest. Movies, TV, magazines and papers flood us with images of these perfect men's bodies. If you believe them, you might find yourself comparing your body to the models or movie heroes ... and coming off second best!

You don't need to compare yourself with some fantasy muscle man on TV. And you don't need to look in the mirror and constantly find your faults either. Ask yourself: why can't I look at the things I like, my strengths and what makes me such a good person? Like the guy's story above, he judged himself as not being OK because he compared himself to a media idea of what a man should be. But when he realised that this is what he'd done, he dug through this and he was able to see his strengths and accept himself.

So you're telling me that exercise makes you happy?

Eating the right type of food isn't the only way to keep healthy. We need to move, dance, walk, ride, skate, swim—anything you like doing that gets your heart pumping in a healthy way. I love sea kayaking—it's fun and I love the water. What do you like doing? Exercise keeps our body fit and healthy and it helps keep us happy. Ever heard of endorphins? Yep, they're happy 'drugs' that are made naturally in the body when we exercise.

BUT, you need to make sure you don't go overboard with exercise or weights. If you lift too many weights too early, you can cause some damage to your muscles and spine. So talk to an expert about this, like your coach or the supervisor at the gym. They'll be able to help you choose an exercise program that suits you.

I felt bad growing up because I compared my body to the mags' ideal of big pecs and six-pack, all aggressive. I'm not like that. I realise now that I had put my strengths away in a rubbish bin because I thought they were not really masculine, not like a real man. I didn't really believe in myself or my strengths. I am now being nothing but who I am. I'm being the real me. It feels like freedom.

the **BRAIN SHIFT**

... boy thinking to young man thinking

'Are we there yet?'... I bet you've asked this question a million times from the back seat of the car. Well, at puberty, you're the one in the front seat and behind the steering wheel of your life, so the answer is really up to you. So, you ask, how do I know when I've arrived at being a young man? It's true your body does change without you thinking about it. But even more important is that your brain becomes capable of thinking and acting differently to a boy's. Just as your testicles become capable of making sperm, your brain becomes capable of new, more adult, thoughts.

The new capability doesn't mean that the thinking shift happens automatically, you'll still have to change the gears! It takes some years of growth and getting serious living experience, but the earlier you decide to start to make the thinking shift, the earlier you can start to enjoy the journey.

If you think **this shift in the way you think is the most important transition for boys, you're right**. Not only is this shift crucial for you personally (because you can't become a healthy man without it!), can you imagine how much trouble a community would be in if none of its boys developed into healthy men? That's right—you and your friends are vital to our community because **you are the next generation of men**.

I can hear you asking already, 'what does that mean?'.

Have you heard of boys in traditional cultures going through an **initiation or rites of passage** before being declared men? For thousands of years in all communities, adults have helped boys make the transition in thinking and behaving (right when their brain is ready for it!) by putting boys through a process of initiation or rite of passage. Not like peer initiations at school or behind the sheds. This is where boys separated from their mothers and went with the men to make ceremonies, face challenges, and learn about manhood. When you think of these rites of passage you may think of circumcision, having a tooth knocked out, cutting or marking boys somehow, or the challenge of being sent out to hunt a lion, or sit with only water for days! These were the kind of challenges the men gave boys to help them make the shift and feel like young men.

But becoming a man was never simply a matter of having your foreskin cut off (thank goodness I hear some of you say!). Boys can't just have the cut and then say, 'Hey, I'm a man'. The most important thing was and is the shift in the heart and the mind of the boy, the giving and taking. The idea is that the cut should remind the boy of the learning experience he went through. **The main part of initiations or rites of passage is to teach boys what is important about healthy manhood.** A bit like going to a manhood school. Sometimes the boys went away with the men for five years to learn about being a man, not seeing their mother in that time.

Your brain has a growth spurt too!

Before we find out what those shifts are, let me tell you something amazing about your brain. That's the 1½ kilo (3 lb) blob of grey matter between your ears. It's running speed is busiest in your childhood, it's flat out. Up to about age 9 or 10 your brain runs at about twice the speed of an adult and it's mainly interested in differences (we learn by being tuned in to differences), emotions and making sense of what's happening around you.

Around age 9 or 10 peer relationships start to dominate your thinking. Your brain starts to change down gears for adolescence. That's right, down the gears, it actually runs slower. Some people jokingly say it stops altogether during age 15! Working on the 'use it or lose it' principle, from about 10 through puberty your brain gets rid of the connections that don't get used much and beefs up the connections that carry the most messages. Your brain potential is not set at birth! Your mental powers get a new chance to grow throughout your teen years. Cells that fire together, wire together!

That's why what you think about during this stage is important.

After early adolescence, the last bit of your brain to mature, the frontal lobes, are getting it together. They are starting to tune up so you are capable of doing **adult things** like plan, consider, control impulses, make wise judgments and be a kind, caring and considerate person. Even emotional maturity—did I hear you say, whatever!?!

Your brain is learning a new set of survival skills based around emotions, forward planning and logical rational thought. During this time you actually need **more sleep** and plenty of **good food** to fuel the changes.

So, while your brain still has its frontal lobe learner plates on, you need adults around to hold the ground while you experiment with being a young man. Puberty is the time when your newly renovated frontal lobes are naturally starting to look out for, and be capable of making sense of, the shifts from boy thinking to young man thinking.

Five thinking shifts to make

Your brain is getting ready to soak them up, the more you think about them the better your brain handles the ideas! So here are the thinking shifts that have been passed down to Puberty Boys by male elders for ages.

Boy thinking	Healthy young man thinking
I'm Mummy's boy	I take responsibility for myself
I'm the centre of the world	The world doesn't revolve around me
I do things to belong with other boys	I enjoy belonging, but I do things because they are right for me
I do risky things to prove myself	I test self-mastery by healthy challenge
I'm special and I'll live forever	I realise I will die

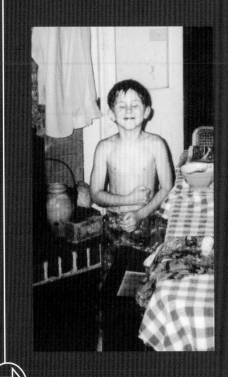

'But all right then, so how do I do it?' I hear you say.

When I've taken boys and their fathers on wilderness rites of passage camps, we work on three practical manhood principles: **responsibility, respect** and **awareness**. The good news is that thinking about, and putting these three ideas into practice, is how you can help hardwire them in your brain and make the five thinking shifts. Only you can make the shifts, nobody can do it for you! So let's take a look at each one of these three principles.

1. Responsibility—or response-ability

The first principle is responsibility, that's being able to respond, do stuff, make things happen, decide, manage, be in charge, and be answerable for and to yourself.

Right now, other people, like your mum and dad probably do many things for you ... like cooking, cleaning, driving you to your friend's place or to training, making decisions, supporting you in many ways, and doing a million other big and little things. Your mum especially probably looks after many personal things for you. This means these people are taking a lot of responsibility for you.

The trick is to do more for yourself, think more for yourself, do what you say you will, and take responsibility for your actions (like owning up to kicking the footy into the best vase in the house rather than saying 'It wasn't me'). It's about becoming more and more independent, separating bit by bit, and staying emotionally close to your mum, dad and other carers.

You may find yourself getting stroppy with your mum, or notice her more often getting cross or fed-up with you, or needing space from you. It's a sign that things are working just as they should! A sign that's asking you to be more responsible for yourself.

Another sign of needing space from parents is wanting to spend more time away from home and with your mates.

Being more independent does not mean we don't need to be looked after by our mum and dad. In fact we may need it more in challenging times. We need to stay emotionally close to our parents so we can receive their support and tell them what is happening for us. It's not a clean break, it's a process that takes years, where you will function more and more without your parents' help, but with their emotional support, so that you can grow independent.

HEALTHY INDEPENDENCE HELPS A PUBERTY BOY TAKE ON THE NUMBER 1 TASK IN BECOMING A YOUNG MAN ... YOU GUESSED IT ... TO TAKE RESPONSIBILITY. THIS IS THE FOUNDATION OF BEING A MATURE YOUNG ADULT, A SELF-RESPONSIBLE PERSON WHO CAN LOOK AFTER HIMSELF EMOTIONALLY AND PHYSICALLY.

I need a break from Mum—when I get angry about boy stuff that she wouldn't necessarily understand ... like I'd come back from footy and all this crap happened on the field. Mum would say don't worry about it, but Dad would say 'that ref was really bad'.

At times my best emotional support is from my mum, it might not be from my dad, depending on what it is ... but sometimes I need a break from one or both of them.

I really miss my mum more than my dad. I'm never thinking she doesn't understand, mums always understand ... even when they're wrong they're right.

I love my mum to death. My parents have just been divorced, but I went on a camp with my dad and other boys with their dads into the bush. We made camp fires, lived off the land, sat in talking circles with other boys and fathers ... we talked about men's things ... it's not secrets from Mum, just private between us men.

Blah, blah, blah, you say, what's in it for me?

There is a huge pay-off for taking responsibility for yourself: you'll get privileges and feel good about yourself. You'll find that the more responsibility you take, the more you can ask for and will be given privileges, like being allowed to spend more time away from home with your friends, staying out later at night, going to parties, or doing your own thing away from your family. You don't just have a right to all this, you need to earn it by taking responsibility and doing what you say you will. Building trust is like building a sandcastle, it takes a long time to make it, and only one wave to come and knock it down! So you need to take care of the trust you build and not wreck it by one silly act.

Taking responsibility needs to be different things in different areas of your life. Let's look at different ways you can start to take responsibility right now.

Pulling your weight

This could be seeing what needs doing at your place and getting it done, maybe without even mentioning it or expecting a reward. It could be making agreements with your family about doing your share of chores, keeping your room clean, doing your washing, cooking a meal, helping in the garden or washing up the dishes. This is about taking the initiative and doing what you've agreed to.

Looking after yourself

Keeping clean, looking after your body and its health, like: cleaning your teeth, cutting your nails, washing properly, exercising, eating healthy not junk food, taking the right clothes for the expected weather when you go out, not smoking, not getting too much sun and getting enough rest.

I'm maturing more, I'm starting to want to go out with my friends, and I don't want to spend time with my family so much any more. But then you come back and say, well, they are my family, I've got to do something with them. It's fun, the family respects you more for going out and seeing a movie with your friends.

Making decisions

Making decisions is about being more involved in discussions and moving towards deciding for yourself what you want to do, what you're interested in, where you want to go, what sport to play, choosing your clothes, how you'll get to your friend's place or the movies, what subjects you're into at school, earning pocket money and deciding who you want to spend time with.

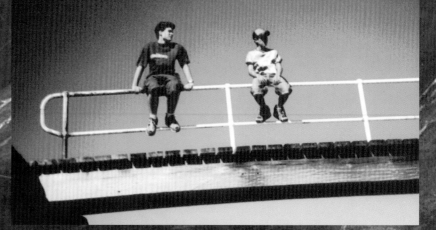

Actions and conduct

This is about, for example, taking more care not to lose or damage things that you or your family own. Showing respect to other people and being thoughtful about what you and other people might need. Admitting or owning up to it when you've done something wrong or made a mistake and doing what's needed to put things right or apologising for any hurt you might have caused. Apologies might go something like: 'I am sorry about the way I ...' or 'I am sorry for saying ...'

I can remember when I first felt I was an independent thinking person. It was an incident with my aunty over a new record player she had, and I knew exactly how to work it, and she came in she just blew her top at me ... and I just stood there thinking, she's just blown her top at me and she's got no reason and I'm fine with this. But before, I would have been really upset by her attack. From then on I had this sense that I was an adult. I look back on that and realise that's when I discovered that I could make a choice about how I react to a situation.

Being in charge of your feelings

You're in charge of your feelings, they're not in charge of you, so you need to think calmly and care about how best to respond to feelings. You also need to think how other people might feel and be affected by your actions before you do them. So, for example, before you throw a temper tantrum, try to imagine what effect this is going to have: is kicking and screaming REALLY going to get your mum to agree to let you go to the movies, or is it likely to make her want to say a big fat NO and send you back to clean your room?

83

The whole lot

A mature guy grows to take responsibility for everything in his life, from his relationships with other people to caring for the environment. Responsibility should grow slowly until you can take responsibility for every aspect of your life by the time you're an adult. A mature guy doesn't blame others or act without caring for things or others. So being responsible is not about picking up a piece of rubbish or doing something the right way, only when others are looking. It's about what we do when no-one is watching, when you have only yourself to answer to. That's the real test.

What do you get out of taking responsibility?

When you can do this—take responsibility for yourself—you'll be self-sufficient, which means that you'll have more self-respect, self-confidence and the feeling of power and ability in your life. The more responsibility you take, the more respect, assistance and trust you will receive from others and the more you'll be allowed and encouraged to do what you want to do.

2. Respect

The second principle is respect, which is acting towards others, yourself (and the natural world) with esteem, honour, consideration and regard. It's about recognising and honouring other people's values, wishes and rights. Realising that you are not the centre of the world, that the world does not revolve around you, can be a bit of a shock. However, this helps you to start being more aware of other people's rights, needs and what they might need from you.

Because our life is about us, it's natural for us to think we're the centre of the world! But the world doesn't centre around any one of us, we're all part of a much bigger picture.

A boy may think that his parents exist only to look after him, that other people's only job is to make him happy. That's Boy thinking. There's an old saying that a boy needed to 'be knocked off his horse' ... that means brought down to earth from his childish idea that the world and other people will forever devote themselves to making him happy.

A boy 'on his horse' wants to take as much as he can for himself. A man can set his own limits. On his horse a boy wants everything right now, off his horse he can wait for things and save for later. On his horse what he wants is most important, off the horse he realises that others have needs too and he respects them. On the horse it is all about taking, off the horse it's about balancing the taking and giving.

Getting off your horse means realising and accepting that the world is imperfect, disappointing and that you are not in control. That can be hard for a boy to swallow!

Being a healthy young man means balancing respect for others with respect for yourself. We need to ask ourselves what it is that we really need. If we don't ever ask this of ourselves, we can't really say that we're respecting ourselves.

Knowing what you need and valuing this is not being selfish, in fact it's the opposite. When you value and respect yourself, you can really

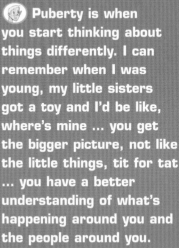 **Puberty is when you start thinking about things differently. I can remember when I was young, my little sisters got a toy and I'd be like, where's mine ... you get the bigger picture, not like the little things, tit for tat ... you have a better understanding of what's happening around you and the people around you.**

I was about 12, I used to steal things like felt-tipped pens, small items, not stuff I really needed. So what was it about? It was the year when I was separated from my father. There wasn't a lot to do, no sport to be done, so we'd go and do something for the thrill of it! I did this with a friend of mine, so that someone would know about it and we could brag about it together. I look back on it and I think how ridiculous.

grow, and in time become capable of being there for others and giving what you have back to your community.

So what might be some things you can do when you live with respect?

◎ Act in ways that make you feel proud of yourself.
◎ Respect the safety and needs of girls.
◎ Take care of your own rubbish, and care for the environment.
◎ Value other people's rights, wishes and property.
◎ Set limits on the things you want.

3. Awareness

Awareness means being watchful, awake, informed, alert, attentive, able to understand and appreciate what's going on in us, for others and around us.

The third principle is awareness. When we have awareness of ourself, we can figure out what we are doing and why we're doing it. Why is this important you ask? Because being aware gives us the chance to make choices that are respectful of ourself, rather than running on autopilot, being ultra-macho, taking crazy risks, being ultra-cool or doing dangerous things to get peer approval, status or belong with a group.

I was unsure of myself, but what helps now is friendships with people that don't care about that. Now I do what I'm good at and like, they just like me as I am.

There are two questions every Puberty Boy needs to ask himself: 'What is important for me to do?' and 'Who is going to come along with me?' If we get those questions in the wrong order we are in trouble. What order do you think they need to be in?

Hey man, take me as I am ...

Having friends and belonging to a peer group outside the family is really, really important. Why? Because it helps us feel like we fit in with others and helps create and reassure our sense of self-worth. But, what we think of ourself, our own self-opinion, is more important because it gives us our own sense of pride.

Your friends won't always be thinking about what's good for you. For example, if your group decides, 'We're going to hang around after school and pick on that boy or that girl', are they really thinking, 'Oh, Jack doesn't like this' or 'Patrick thinks this is a bad idea'? You can bet they're NOT! So this is where your thinking for yourself comes into it. Why should you hurt someone else just to make other people happy? Why should you hurt yourself just to show your friends that you can do something daring or silly?

It is so important for Puberty Boys to feel they belong with their friends that they sometimes take risks and do crazy things to prove they are worthy or tough enough, or to impress or gain status with them. Being rude to adults, acting ultra-tough, getting into fights, drinking, smoking, bullying, stealing, vandalism, slacking off at school or treating girls or women with disrespect are some of the things groups might try to throw at you to prove yourself to them. But think about it for a minute—is being rude and hurting others something you'd like done to you? And is doing these things really YOU?

Healthy Puberty Boys and men don't live their lives just to get admiration and approval from others. Admiration and approval come to them!

Not living your life just to get admiration from other people takes self-respect and inner strength. **Being liked by others is important, but being yourself is more important.** Saying NO when you are asked to do something that is not what you want takes courage.

What worked was having people who accepted me for who I was. I needed that acceptance, not needing it from everybody, but from my small group.

I always had this feeling of having like a secret life, that my family life was 'straight', like a pretend life, a mask for the world, whereas the real life I lived away from home, out on the streets, like being a vandal, roaming the streets at night when I was pretending to be doing homework at another boy's place. At home Mum was boss, outside the door it was another world. I used to hide what I was doing and take care of Mum by pretending. I was very good at acting.

Pushing yourself to the max is OK!

Puberty is a time of taking risks. It's when we need to challenge ourselves to find our limits. But that doesn't mean you need to skate on the highway dodging cars to see how fast you can go! Unfortunately, many Puberty Boys can mistake this need for challenge and do dangerous experiments, alone or with mates, to experience the thrill, the fear and to push the boundary of excitement. That's when being aware of how to challenge yourself in positive ways can really save your butt.

Challenges are part of rites of passage because they give a boy a chance to prove something about himself to himself, to experiment to see what he is capable of. You can create your own challenges, without breaking the law, doing crazy things or putting your neck on the line. It's fantastic to be able to stretch yourself by doing something you've never done before.

Risk is essential for Puberty Boys, because the experience of healthy risk-taking teaches us how far we can go safely and within our own and other people's limits. But before you jump into risky situations ask yourself: If my friends weren't here to watch and I had no-one to impress, would I want to do this? Healthy risk-taking is about developing and testing your self-mastery (that's your ability to successfully command and control yourself to get things done) it's not about impressing your peers! You can take challenges and opportunities in a positive way that won't hurt other people, the environment or you!

Design your own challenge

All over the world Puberty Boys take on amazing healthy challenges (I emphasise that it can't be done without older men supervising!), **like sleeping in a jungle cave with spiders to overcome fear! Face the bush in the dark. Stand up all night to test willpower. Sit for days with only water on a vision quest. Abseil down a cliff to face fear of heights. Navigate out of a wilderness place they don't know.** And many others. All over the world, all of them are done in the company of men who don't interfere, they just make sure nothing goes wrong.

Healthy challenges expand your idea of who you are and create a shift in how you see yourself ... more man than boy. Challenges need to be hard and exciting. The important thing is that it must be about facing your fears or doing a personal best.

Here are some more ideas for adventures you might consider:

◎ Spending a night, or a few days, in nature or wilderness to consider your vision of what is important for you, to consider what are the issues you need to face up to in your life and how you propose to deal with them.
◎ Taking a journey, maybe a long canoe trip or walk.

We used to throw rocks on teachers' roofs and hide in their gardens and the idea is for them to come out and yell and stuff, and for us to be hiding in the cabbages right in front of their feet and as close as possible, just to feel the fear and get a kick out of it ... it was getting that feeling of excitement and testing ourselves.

I encourage you to design your own challenges. Remember these challenges or adventures must be done on your own, but in the company of, and organised with and supervised by, older men. Never take off on your own without telling the adults in your life. This is definitely not a smart thing to do!

Remember our list of shifts, there's just one left to mention. It's a biggie!

Accepting you will die! Don't turn the page, I know it's heavy, but it matters!

It is only when a person can **really** accept that he is going to die, that he can fully live. You don't want to be obsessed by death, but if we are frightened of it, or ignore it, we can find ourselves not fully living. So ask yourself, if you really accept that you are going to die, if you let the fear of it go, if you stopped denying it will happen ... then how would you decide you wanted to live?

The map is not the journey!

So there you go, the five thinking shifts we've talked about in this chapter can be summed up by three words ... **responsibility, respect and awareness.**

After reading this chapter you may be thinking 'You can't tell me to do all that stuff!'. Or maybe you are thinking that's way too much, or it's just a whole lot more stuff adults tell me I have to do. If so, hang on—I'm not saying you have to do this stuff, I am letting you know the difference between Boy thinking and Young Man thinking, the rest is up to you. These ideas are like a map, taking the journey is up to you. Knowing the map is not enough, you have to travel the territory yourself, actually do it.

Remember that **changing from boy to young man happens over time, not overnight**. Sometimes we change deliberately; at others we find ourself doing or thinking differently when we are naturally ready. It's an individual thing. Whenever change is in the air there is always uncertainty. If you feel that, it's normal, in fact necessary ... **boys cannot become men without a period of uncertainty**.

Chapter 11

HELP
does not = WEAK
WEAK

We all need help sometimes

I know from my personal puberty experience that sometimes it takes courage to keep asking questions (I don't mean just at school) or be yourself in front of your peers. Boys sometimes hold back on asking questions, believing HELP means being WEAK. But it takes more courage to ask questions and ask for help than to remain silent!

We all need guidance from time to time, so don't be a butt head, ask for it! There are people all around who can help. Your parents for one, especially your dad. Talk to them, ask them what they think, what they did in a similar situation. You'll be surprised by what you hear!

In fact, a boy may find it difficult to become a healthy man without guidance from, and spending time with, older men. It's hard to become what you've never seen!

When my mother and two sisters are out of the house, it's so quiet and me and my dad just treasure it, 'cause it's so quiet and we can just do anything really, talk about anything.

Dads and mentors

Sometimes dads are around, sometimes not. If you live with your father, or see him frequently, or even infrequently, this is a blessing to take advantage of, if he is open to it. Take the opportunity to ask him about what he's doing, ask him to spend time with you, talk and do things together. He's not a mind reader! Help him out by talking to him about what's going on for you and let him know what you need from him by asking for what you need. For example, if dad's always at work, you need to tell him how that is for you and ask him to spend more time with you. This is another way of taking self-responsibility.

If you don't have a dad, or even if you do, you can find a mentor. Mentors are older people you feel you admire and trust, who will act for your benefit and who you can talk openly to about the challenges in your life. A mentor will not tell you what to do, but help you make your own decisions and maybe he'll have a story from his own life that will help you decide. A mentor can also be someone you don't actually talk to but watch and listen closely to the positive things they say and do. They are good role models for you to copy.

Who can be a mentor—and where do you find them?

A male mentor may be an uncle, neighbour, grandfather, stepfather, friend of your father, coach, teacher, counsellor, family friend, older person at school or someone you know. There are mentoring programs in many schools and organisations. If you have someone in mind, ask a parent or another adult about him before you make any approach.

How do you know if you can trust a mentor?

You should always feel safe with a mentor. It should always feel like he's looking out for you, not himself. He should be a good listener, patient, not judgmental and keep what you say confidential if you ask him to. He should never insist you do something you don't want to do and there should be no hint in him of sexual behaviour or interest in you. If this happens tell another adult immediately.

Boys who have a mentor usually say they feel better about themselves and have more confidence. A mentor (and a parent!) is most effective when he shares with you his experience of an issue facing you, helps you sort out your own feelings and ideas, and talks with you to help you find options for your own way forward and to make your own choices.

Chapter 12

Developing your
EMOTIONAL
INTELLIGENCE
what, do emotions have a brain!?!

You've heard of IQ, that's about intelligence. At puberty one of your biggest challenges is to develop your EQ, **emotional intelligence**. Learning emotional intelligence is like learning to ride a bike. It can seem impossible and weird at first, but if we keep at it, we get the hang of it, start to enjoy it, and soon it becomes second nature and, like a bike, we wonder how we ever got anywhere fast enough without it.

Use it or lose it!

Your puberty brain's frontal lobe is maturing, setting you up to be more emotionally capable. Following the 'use it or lose it' principle, you can develop your emotional intelligence by deciding to focus on your emotions and feelings. I strongly recommend it! However, there's a catch! While their brain is gearing up, boys are mostly taught to tune out and turn their emotions down.

Boys are taught rules about how to be. At puberty we don't even know that we have been taught these because the rules are invisible, but they are like a film script inside us telling us how we must act, and we know it off by heart. By the time we reach puberty we may not even know what's missing. But as boys, we do feel things, it's just that most of us are simply taught not to show it.

Amazingly, up to age 5 or so, we males tend to be more emotionally expressive than girls. Around age 5, TV, movies, video games, parents, teachers and kids in the playground all kick in with messages to boys that they must toughen up. We're told things like 'don't cry' or 'it's only a scratch' or 'don't be a wuss', and the most dreaded one, 'don't be a sissy'. The message is don't show your vulnerability or feelings or you won't be a man. Do of any of these sound familiar?

Getting these messages over and over again as we grow up, and copying what our fathers do, is the most obvious way boys learn to be men. We learn that boys are supposed to be tough, which has a good side. Tough and courageous men do amazing things like fighting a bush fire, going up a live power pole, or working physically hard.

I'm 22 and even talking about feelings, it just pushes itself away and thoughts come that it should go away. I tell myself that I'm being silly. There's lots of messages about feelings not being OK. And instead of being able to feel what they really are … it just goes under the one emotion that's acceptable for blokes, it all comes out as anger. Only sometimes it's not anger, it's hurt, sadness, helplessness or feeling ashamed.

I'm an expert at hiding my true emotions and my true self. When my mother was angry at me I would withdraw, go silent. I hid my anger and other feelings. I became expert at hiding my emotions from her because if she got angry with me I felt like she would cut me off and I would be helpless and no-one would look after me. I put my own needs away and threw myself into my school work in order to be good and receive Mum's approval.

But the macho stuff has a down side. We know the brain works on a 'use it or lose it' basis. These messages boys receive can drive us to cut off our feelings, cut off the ties between feelings and feeling words, so our brain may not develop in the emotions department. We may put away not just vulnerable feelings, but the whole lot. We can end up in touch with only anger, hunger and lust! If we don't develop our feeling words, we can eventually lose touch with our hearts and our inner experience.

There's a boy code of silence ... be silent about our inner world, especially to other boys and men if we want to measure up and belong. This code of silence may reduce our ability to relate deeply to girls too.

The challenge for Puberty Boys is to sense where you are between the two extremes of little boy (their feelings are in charge of them) and ultra-macho (their feelings are far away). The idea is not to be touchy-feely to the max, but to be able to be self-aware enough to be in touch with feelings of all kinds and be able to speak to them at the right time, in the right way, with the right person! The idea is to have enough awareness to be able to choose.

Tell it like it is ...

Puberty is when life gets more complex, when girls, relationships and personal challenges arrive. This is when we need to feel, and be able to find the words for how it is inside and tell those important to us.

It takes more courage to reveal our innermost feelings to ourselves or to others close to us, than to hide them. Tolerating and speaking feelings of 'weakness' or vulnerability can be the most courageous thing a boy or man ever does ... and it has huge rewards, **including that girls love it when we do!**

If I'm sad at school I have to put on a happy face, or else they'd tease me for sure. Show feelings to anyone at school? As if!

Why bother with emotions and this feeling stuff?

If we're out of touch with our feelings, they can take over when we don't want them to. If we can't experience emotions then we can't tell the difference between all the different feelings we're having and we can't put words to them. If we cannot express feelings and connect with others, we risk getting sick or stressed or becoming anxious.

Think of feelings like big signs telling us what is happening inside us, our inner world. If we can't tell, we'd be like hollow men, and not know which way to go. When we can tell, we can think, act and choose taking account of our inner world. That has a big effect on the kind of life we have.

Sometimes I get upset because maths is so hard. One day I was crying and angry at the same time. Mum came in and like always told me to not be so silly, that there was no need to be upset. But I was upset! I pretended to be OK.

FEELING FACES

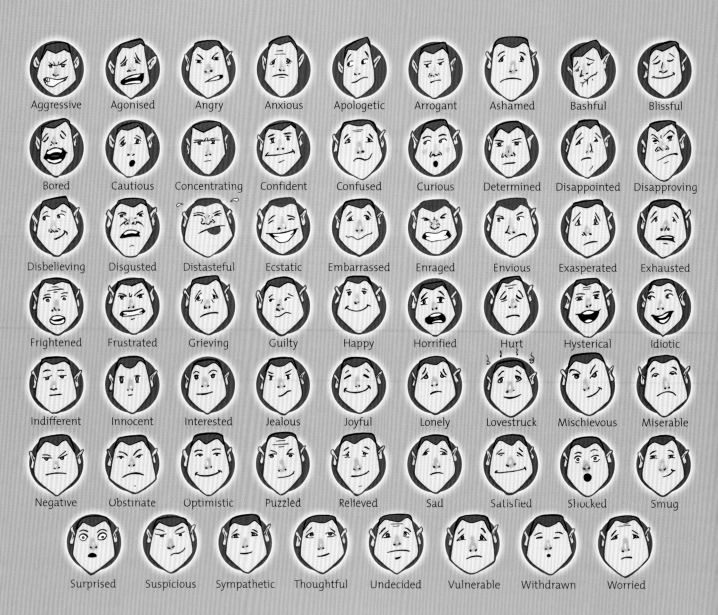

Aggressive	Agonised	Angry	Anxious	Apologetic	Arrogant	Ashamed	Bashful	Blissful
Bored	Cautious	Concentrating	Confident	Confused	Curious	Determined	Disappointed	Disapproving
Disbelieving	Disgusted	Distasteful	Ecstatic	Embarrassed	Enraged	Envious	Exasperated	Exhausted
Frightened	Frustrated	Grieving	Guilty	Happy	Horrified	Hurt	Hysterical	Idiotic
Indifferent	Innocent	Interested	Jealous	Joyful	Lonely	Lovestruck	Mischievous	Miserable
Negative	Obstinate	Optimistic	Puzzled	Relieved	Sad	Satisfied	Shocked	Smug
Surprised	Suspicious	Sympathetic	Thoughtful	Undecided	Vulnerable	Withdrawn	Worried	

The lowdown on finding and dealing with feelings

The first thing to do with feelings is to recognise them in yourself. So, let's get those brain connections happening! First check out the feeling faces drawing on the left. Stand in front of a mirror and make each face yourself. Notice if, or how, your body changes when you become each feeling. Make a habit of looking at your face and other people's faces and practise putting words to the expressions you see. For example, 'I feel angry when you come and wake me up when I am still trying to sleep.'

Next check out your body—it is a telltale sign of your feelings. Usually your feelings will be held in your body trunk—that's between your groin and neck. By focusing on sensations, like butterflies, tension, hot or cold, tingling, blushing or tummy churning, you can learn to get in touch with different feelings and to put words to them. I invite you to practise this every day.

If you've noticed a feeling, what do you do with it?

Suppress it?

Suppressing emotions means bottling it all up. This can make us feel tense, stressed and physically sick. When we never tell anyone how we feel we can become lonely and it's hard for anyone to really know us and be true friends.

Explode?

The other extreme is **exploding**, for example, with anger. This can feel like losing control. It may let off steam but it might be the wrong place and time, and might frighten or push others away and make you feel guilty later. It's not a bad thing to feel anger, because anger itself is not a bad emotion. It's what we do with it that matters. Suppressing emotions is like putting the lid back on top of a shaken-up coke bottle and waiting for it to explode.

I'm 14, but not telling people how I'm feeling ... like keeping heaps of things bottled up ... keeping it all in and not telling anybody, and then I feel miserable and I don't think I can handle it. Then I think bad things about myself.

103

There are better ways than suppressing and exploding

Contain it

Containing is breathing deeply, releasing some tension by acknowledging the feeling and pressing the 'hold' button inside your head. Containing is holding the emotion, knowing what it is, and choosing not to make it public or share it right now. This is a good first step and can help you feel confident enough to deal with conflict. It also helps reduce stress.

Express it

Expressing is getting the feeling out, speaking it calmly or wildly, laughing it, even crying it sometimes. Letting it out can help you feel relieved—like a huge sigh—and it also helps other people to understand you.

Dealing with sadness and depression

Puberty is a time when we might have pressures and conflict with parents, brothers and sisters, friends, at school or face stressful situations, struggle with confusion, down feelings and moods. All this can happen at a time when we haven't had enough experience to know how to handle it. We can feel anxious, stressed, sad or down. It's natural that this happens to some of us, for short periods of time, during puberty. It's worse when it goes on for a long time and when we think we can't talk to anyone about it (that's sometimes called being depressed).

We can avoid thinking traps

Ben usually had trouble with his exams. He decided that if he couldn't do well, it would be a bad thing that would ruin the rest of his life. And so Ben felt he was the problem, and he told himself that he was stupid and became anxious.

   Ben could rethink things this way: Exams are hard, I really need to get more coaching if I want to pass them.

Will had a fight with someone at school who is now upset with him and not friendly. He decided that everybody hated him and that he should leave school.

Will could rethink the situation this way: OK, we've had a fight, do I want to stay friends with him? If yes, then how can we make up? If no, then I've got others around to be friends with.

Sometimes bad things do happen to us, but mostly, the events that happen to us are not the real problem! It's the way we decide to explain them that is the real problem. Yes, you have the power to look at things in a more positive way—you can do it! ... and when you can do it, the sadness or depressing feelings will go away.

Trap 1. Explaining a situation by blaming ourself. For example, when we have a misunderstanding with a friend, and we see ourselves as the problem, as not OK, instead of seeing the misunderstanding as the problem. This can make us feel sad or depressed.

Trap 2. Is to explain the situation in wrong and unhelpful ways like:
◎ **I must** ... Telling myself I must be perfect or else I'm an idiot. Or other people must always be friendly or else I'm not OK.
◎ **One event makes the rule.** If one person doesn't like me, everyone will hate me too. This is absolutely not true.
◎ **Unreal predictions.** If I fail this exam my life is ruined. Some of the most successful men in our times have failed some exams!

Chapter 13

Hints for
RELATING
with **GIRLS**

So you want to be interesting, get attention and create friendships with girls?

The first thing is to remember that girls are going through a similar stage in their life, just like you are. So if you're feeling unsure of yourself, then they probably are feeling the same way. Girls might appear more secure to you, but most girls will be very sensitive about their body shape, how it's changing and how they look. Everyone can feel uncertain and unsure of themselves during puberty, it's not just you.

But all right, you want some hints on how to talk to girls?

I can remember the first time I asked a girl out to a school dance. The two things I remember most are that she accidentally slammed my finger in the car door and that I couldn't think of a sensible thing to say to her all night. We didn't go out again! Not surprising.

I've never had a problem with girls, they're cuties, like since I was 8 I've liked girls. I used to like toys and fads and Pokemon and stuff up to when I was about 11, then I just got rid of them. I'm not interested in them now but in stuff that lasts a little longer ... like a little happy meal toy lasts 2 seconds and dogs come and eat it, girls last longer.

Here's what you can do to talk to girls:

◎ **Get to know your feelings:** By developing self-awareness of your inner, feeling world, you will have something of yourself to share with girls aside from surfing, sports, cars and stuff like that.

◎ **Lots of shared feelings:** Girls talk to each other about not just what happens but how they feel about what happens. A good way into a conversation with girls when things happen is to ask, 'how did you feel when ...' and then share with her how you felt and why.

◎ **Show sensitivity:** If you can be sensitive and respectful to what might be going on for a girl, and showing it by genuinely asking questions about how she is, it will go a long way to showing her you are caring enough about her to warrant her attention and trust.

◎ **Have fun:** Girls appreciate a sense of humour.

◎ **Talking one on one:** Boys love it when girls approach them and girls would love it if boys did the same to them. This can be tricky if you get caught up in a group. You can be pulled in two directions, one way is belonging and looking cool in your peer group, the other way is risking leaving the group to go and talk to a girl one to one.

◎ **Be aware of what message you're sending:** Sometimes Puberty Boys in a group can appear to be more interested in making sure they appear cool and belong to their group than interested in a girl. A girl can get confused about your feelings with all the mixed messages you might be giving off. For example, you might talk to her differently when you're with a group of friends and this might cause confusion.

◎ **Don't let others' teasing get in the way:** If your group tease you when they see you with a girl or put you down in front of her, then you might need to act independently of your group for a while.

◎ **Listen ... and talk:** Girls are taught to **relate**. If you want to relate to a girl you have to be able to tell her about yourself and give her the opportunity to do the same with you. That means you have to listen so she will talk, and talk so she will listen.

Hints for conversation starters (and restarters)

1. **Ask a question about her or see if you can help her do something.** For example: 'What's going on with you today?' or 'How would you feel about going to the movies later?' or 'What are you looking for? How can I help?' If you run out of things to say questions are great conversation restarters.

2. **Find out if you have anything in common.** Ask a girl if she is into interests and subjects that you like. Ask/find out hers.

3. **Put her at ease, let her know you appreciate her, and comment on an aspect of her you like.** Perhaps something like: 'You look really cool today, great clothes' (don't say this if she's in school uniform!) or 'I've been looking forward to talking with you' or 'I like the way you do that'. Don't make it up, only say what you really believe.

4. **Tell her some news or comment on the situation.** Some examples are: 'Did you hear what happened yesterday at the shops?' or 'I heard something amazing today ...'

5. **Avoid conversation blockers.** Don't talk about yourself all the time. Talk about yourself when asked. And don't boast, big-note, brag, exaggerate, or try to be what you're not. Rude comments or teasing won't help you win her over either.

6. **Save up and memorise interesting things you hear.** If you hear something on television or radio that you like, or if you read it in a book or newspaper, write it down. But you don't want to sound like a copycat so try to make it your own somehow.

 A girl used to come into my father's shop. It took me weeks to figure out how to ask her to the school dance. Amazingly, she said yes, and the big night came. I found a way to say 'hello' at the start of the night and 'goodnight' at the end. That's all the conversation I could make for the whole night ... so if you can think of more things to say than that you're doing really well!

FIND a COMMON INTEREST

TALK AND LISTEN

RESPECT EACH OTHER

Chapter 14

FIGHT, RUN ...or a 3rd way?

A tough teen, about 14, told me this story ...

I've learnt you don't have to be, what's the word—a stereotype—to come across as being strong. I don't have to act strong, what it boils down to is how adult I can be. Which I found out last Friday at school. Sitting with my girlfriend and some friends, I went away and when I came back there was a guy sitting next to her. My friend said get rid of him, I could feel myself getting angry about it, 'cause if he was angry then I knew it was serious, because he's a pretty tough sort of guy. I was really rattled. I could feel it rising in me, but I got rid of it and then I walked up and said 'Oh, s'cuse me mate I just want to sit next to her'. He moved out of the way, I sat down next to her and she said, 'Thank you so much for doing that, he was really bugging me'. My first thought was to react violently, but I turned that off completely and sat down and just handled it perfectly. I was so proud, really proud of myself, I've been ready to fight at the drop of a hat so many times before. Even my friend said nice one, so I was doubly proud.

This story tells us of a big challenge for any Puberty Boy, that is, to manage what he does when there is conflict, threat, danger, situations he doesn't like, or when he becomes angry. The most important thing is to remember that you have a **choice**.

AGGRESSIVE	ASSERTIVE	PASSIVE
Fight	Stand	Run
Macho/Bully	Warrior	Wimp
Anger	Calm	Fear
Uncertain	Confident	Uncertain

The choice at the macho end is **aggression** and that's not OK, except to protect yourself or protect others.

At the other end is being **passive**—that's being unable to stand up for yourself or ask directly for what you want. This may be a good tactic once in a while, but if you are passive all the time you won't win the friends or respect that you may hope for. Instead, people will come to pity or disrespect you.

In the middle is the 3rd way, and that is being **assertive**, which means being strong enough to know what you need and be able to stand, handle yourself, and speak up for yourself and others without being either a bully (aggressive) or a wimp (passive).

Forget blaming testosterone for making us aggressive. It's a myth and it's just a cop out for not taking responsibility for how we choose to act.

Anger is not a bad thing!

Anger is an important, valuable emotion. It can let us know when we are threatened or our boundaries are being crossed, so it's like a signpost emotion telling us to pay attention. But, anger can also cover over other emotions like sadness, shame, hurt, fear or feeling powerless, and if it does, we need to dig through it to find out what is really happening for us. That way we don't make the mistake of hitting someone angrily when we're actually feeling low about something. It happens! Some guys, when they feel sad or low, go out and pick a fight! You need to be aware of this to help you not fall into this trap.

ANGER

FEAR
SADNESS
HURT
SHAME
HELPLESSNESS

Anger is not violence. But acting out anger with violence is not OK. Exploders need to learn to contain emotions sometimes. Suppressors need to learn to express emotions sometimes.

It is OK to be confronting when necessary to protect yourself or others who need your help. It's not wise to rush into action without first stepping back to make sure that your action is called for, your purpose is good and clear, and the consequences are considered. A healthy young man is no bully, he doesn't pick on others, he prefers to work with and influence others rather than conquer or manipulate them. That's what I mean by the **3rd way**.

A boy has something to prove about himself. He's full of ego and wind, he gets into fights to prove something, like how tough he is, because he is actually unsure of himself and doesn't know how to be anything but macho.

A healthy man makes up his own mind about what is worth fighting for, based on what he believes is right and worthwhile.

Teasing is teasing ...

For many boys, teasing can be a way to express feelings they can't say directly. Like the way Cartman's friends call him 'lard ass' on South Park, when he's obviously overweight. Or the way shorter guys are sometimes nicknamed 'short stuff'. They might think this is showing affection through teasing, but the words can really hurt our feelings, and it might make us feel put down and criticised. If this is how you show affection to people, don't you think you'll keep your friends better if you learn to show your affection directly?

I'm not a bully ... I'm just made that way!

Some teasers and bullies who deliberately pick on others, don't care about other people's feelings. Some people feel bad about bullying if they see they've hurt someone, and they don't repeat it. But ringleaders who keep doing it are different, they start it and keep it going.

These bullies pick on people who are vulnerable, weak, or who are scared of being a victim. They often know those feelings well because they usually feel them too.

A bully may have been picked on himself, so he picks on those weaker than him to avoid his own bad feelings about himself. A person might bully others to get status, attention, belong, be popular, or act so tough that he won't be attacked. They often don't know how to relate to people.

Harsh words, threats, manipulation, exclusion, put downs, name calling, teasing or violence like pushing, shoving or punching is all bullying. Could this be you?

If you do bully others, it's time to become self-aware about what you are doing and why you are doing it. Ask yourself, **'What am I trying to get by bullying?'** It's hard to see ourselves as others do, so you'll probably need adult help with pinpointing this in yourself. It's worth doing, if you don't it may dog you for life. It's time to find a non-abusive way, to get what you are really looking for.

Defending yourself if attacked or bullied

If you are attacked, bullied or involved in a conflict, here's what you need to remember:

◎ In conflict the first thing to do is to maintain self-control of your feelings, body and thoughts. The old EQ comes in handy here! If you lose it you might become more vulnerable to a bully.

◎ Violence is not the best option. But if you need to defend yourself you must decide what is worth fighting for and assess the odds of coming out on top. Sometimes it is smarter tactics to walk away or refuse to fight.

◎ The number one thing to do is to let the bully know that you want his or her behaviour to stop. You can do this by standing up for yourself, being assertive and expressing your opinion in a calm but firm way. Have your friends stand by you in a positive way. You don't have to stand up to a bully alone.

◎ Remember that asking for help when you need it is not weak, but a sign of security and strength. There may be times when a bully is bigger or stronger than you and will not let up. If you can't physically do anything about it or fight back, don't close your eyes and pretend it isn't happening because that only encourages a bully. Asking for help is the smart thing to do in this situation, so talk to parents, teachers, school counsellors or mentors about the problem.

◎ When threatened, the impression you give to others when they look at you is crucial to how they react to you. Even if you're not sure of yourself

you need to hold your chin up, chest forward but not puffed up, shoulders back and relaxed, make eye contact but don't stare or overdo it as this can seem aggressive. Try to keep your voice clear and calm.

◎ If you are defending yourself when attacked physically or verbally, your object is not to hurt the other person, but to do only enough to prevent getting hurt yourself.

Puberty—steps in your journey to manhood

Puberty is part of a journey, steps in the adventure of life we all take. Your life will be largely what you make it, you have a choice about which paths to take and what kind of man you will be. Boys are born, men are made. Awareness is the key—awareness of yourself and the choices you can make. My hope is that *Puberty Boy* will help you know yourself better, inside and out, so that you can have a fantastic start on your journey to manhood. Walk easy.

Puberty Boy has a website. You can check it out at http://www.allenandunwin. com/pubertyboy.asp.

GLOSSARY

acne Inflammation of the sebaceous glands of the skin

adolescence Transition period between puberty and adulthood

aggressive Attacking, hostile, offensive; assault verbally or physically

assertive Be strong, honest, truthful; speak up for yourself; ask for what you need

awareness Being watchful, awake, informed, attentive; understand and appreciate

bulbourethral gland Reproductive gland, produces pre-cum slippery fluid

cervix Opening at top of female vagina into uterus

circumcision Removal of foreskin covering head of the penis

clitoris Female pleasure spot

condom Contraceptive sheath for male penis

contraception Deliberate methods to prevent conception (pregnancy)

corona Ridge around the head of the penis where it meets the shaft

depression Feeling sad, down, not OK, glum, unmotivated for more than a few weeks

emotional intelligence Ability to experience, name, express and manage feelings

epididymis Organ at rear of testicle in which sperm mature

ejaculation Rhythmic muscle contractions to spurt semen from the penis

ejaculatory ducts Reproductive glands

erection Penis when erect, hardened by blood pumped into penis

fallopian tubes Female reproductive tubes, from where eggs travel to the uterus

flaccid Describes the usual state of penis, soft, droopy or limp

foreskin Loose skin covering head of uncircumcised penis

frenulum Sensitive skin on underside of penis where head meets the shaft

gay man A male homosexual

genes Unit of inheritance, carries characteristics from parent to child

genitals Male and female reproductive organs

glans Head of the penis

gonads Male and female primary sex organs. Testicles and ovaries

homophobia Fear or hatred of other men, especially gay men

hormones Substances which activate organs into action e.g. testosterone

independence Self dependence and reliance; doing or thinking more for yourself

initiation Ceremony to teach, admit and welcome boys into a community of men

libido Male and female sex drive or desire for sex

macho man One who is over the top being tough, stoic, aggressive and strong

masturbation Self-stimulation of the genitals resulting in ejaculation

menarche A girl's first menstrual period

mentor Older, trusted, respected person to talk to, who can wisely guide and assist

ovary Female primary sex organ, stores and sends eggs after puberty starts

passive Submitting; wimpy; not speaking up or standing up for yourself

peer group People of about the same age or situation

penis Male organ of urination and reproduction

perineum Diamond shaped area between the pubic bone and anus

periods Female monthly menstrual cycle, menstruation

prostate Gland producing fluid for semen, muscles inside it contract during ejaculation

puberty Age of attaining sexual maturity and being able to reproduce

pubes Hair appearing on lower abdomen at puberty

respect Thinking and acting with esteem, honour, consideration and regard

responsibility Your ability to think act, manage, respond and be in charge of yourself

rite of passage Ceremony to mark a change of status, e.g. from boy to man

safety network A circle of people you trust, can rely on, ask for help and talk to

scrotum Pouch of skin that contains your testicles

self-mastery Ability to successfully command and control yourself

semen Fluid expelled at ejaculation, contains sperm

seminal vesicles Reproductive glands

sexual intercourse (sex) Insertion of the penis into vagina followed by ejaculation

spermatozoa (sperm) Male reproductive cell or 'tadpole', made in testicles

stereotype Standard idea of something, e.g. usual idea of how a man must be

STI Sexually transmitted infection

testicles Balls in your scrotum that produce hormones and sperm

urethra Tube from bladder to exterior, carries urine and semen

uterus Womb, place in woman where fertilised egg implants and baby grows

vagina Female sex organ, passage from the uterus to the vulva

virgin/virginity Person (or state of a person) who has not had sexual intercourse

vulva External area of female genitals

wet dream Ejaculation that happens when asleep

HANDY RESOURCES

Help for kids

If you need some help with a problem, or if you're feeling sad or lonely, there are many places you can call for help. The people there are trained to listen and help you.

Kids Helpline free call: 1800 551 800. This is a help service for kids of any age, up to 18 years. It's a 24 hour service. Or on the web: http://www.kidshelp.com.au

Lifeline phone: 13 114 or on the web: http://www.lifeline.org.au/

Eating Disorders Support Network phone: 02 9412 4499 or on the web: http://www.edsn.asn.au

Young People in NSW: http://www.kids.nsw.gov.au/

Body Positive looks at having a positive body image and feeling good about the bodies we have. On the web: http://www.bodypositive.com/

Puberty websites

Sex, etc. is a newsletter for teens by teens around sexuality on the web: http://www.sxetc.org

Virtual Kid Puberty has got 101 answers to questions regarding changes in your body. On the web: http://www.virtualkid.com

This website has a lot of information and covers many subjects—prepared by young people: www.headroom.net.au/lounge/framejamming_lounge.html

Teen Health—answers and advice on the web: http://www.kidshealth.org/kid/

Sexually Transmitted Infections—here are two websites to check out for information: www.niaid.nih.gov/factsheets/stdinfo.htm and www.sexualityandu.ca/eng/teens/STI

Rites of passage

Pathways to Manhood is a fantastic award-winning program that involves a five-day camp centred around a rite of passage. It is attended by boys and their fathers (or an appropriate male mentor). The aim of Pathways is to bring out the potential in young men and have them full of hope and inspiration as they look to the future. Phone: (02) 6684 3392 or on the web: www.pathwaysfoundation.com.au/

Mentoring

Mentoring Association of Australia official website: www.dsf.org.au/mentor/links.htm

e-Mentor pro is a specialised emailing utility, which provides a highly secure method for school children to develop a fixed-term mentoring email relationship with a range of volunteer adults in the community. On the web: http://www.e-mentoring.com.au/

Big Brother Big Sister website: www.ywca-sydney.com.au/bsbb/

Uncle Project is a mentoring and activities program (on the Far North Coast of NSW) for local boys without active fathers. This is a community-based organisation committed to guiding and supporting young boys in their personal development during a challenging period of their lives. The Uncle Team phone: (02) 6680 8582, postal address: Byron Bay NSW 2481, on email: info@uncle.org.au and on the web: http://www.uncle.org.au/

Talk It Up is a website (by the Australian Broadcasting Corporation) about health, strength, happiness and growing into adulthood. It is designed to connect young people across urban and regional Australia, at school or after hours, in a safe online environment. Web: http://www.abc.net.au/talkitup/

Face-to-face help

Geoff Price—Talkitover provides counselling for male teens, adults and couples, specialising in men and relationships. Phone: (02) 9416 7563, email: geoff@talkitover.info and on the web: www.talkitover.info

Health, nutrition and wellbeing sites

The Child and Youth Health for South Australia website has a section on puberty: www.cyh.com.au

ReachOut has lots of youth health factsheets, through the Inspire Foundation. It's also a cool place to chill out and clear your head on the web: http://www.reachout.com.au/

INDEX